C.F.A.VOYSEY an architect of individuality

on or before

Duncan Simpson

C·F·A·VOYSEY

an architect of individuality

with a preface by Sir James Richards

Lund Humphries · London

First edition 1979
Published by
Lund Humphries Publishers Ltd
26 Litchfield Street London WC2

SBN 85331 426 8

Designed by Herbert Spencer
Filmset by Keyspools Ltd, Golborne, Lancs
Printed and bound by Lund Humphries, Bradford, Yorks

Frontispiece: A contemporary photograph, *c.* 1900, showing
Voysey in his work-room or study at his house,
The Orchard, at Chorleywood.

Cover illustrations: Walnut Tree Farm (9b) and The Homestead (61)

Photographic acknowledgements

Copyright The Royal Institute of British Architects, London: frontispiece, 1, 5, 9c, 11, 13, 14, 16, 17,
18, 19, 20a, 22, 28, 29c, 29d, 30a, 30b, 31, 32, 33a, 33b, 34, 37, 40, 41, 45a, 45b, 47b, 56b, 62, 64, 65, 66,
67, 68, 69
Copyright Royal Pavilion, Art Gallery and Museums: 2, 7a, 7b, 8b, 9a, 9b, 10, 14b, 14c, 20b, 20c,
20d, 20f, 21a, 21b, 21c, 26, 29b, 29e, 29f, 29g, 29i, 30d, 30e, 30f, 30g, 30h, 35a, 38a, 38b, 38c, 38d,
39, 43, 46a, 46b, 47a, 48, 50, 53, 70, 73
Copyright *Country Life*: 44, 61
Copyright Portsmouth City Art Gallery: 51
Copyright Victoria and Albert Museum: 30c
Copyright Whitworth Art Gallery: 71

All other photographs remain the copyright of the author.

Contents

Preface

by Sir James Richards

I met C.F.A.Voysey only once and then I said the wrong thing. The year was 1938; so Voysey must have been eighty-one. I called on him at his flat in St James's and found him a slight, sharp-featured figure dressed wholly in blue, courteous but not very forthcoming. My mistake was to acknowledge that I was specially interested in talking to him at that moment because of a Penguin book I was writing on modern architecture in which he appeared among those who had pioneered the break-away from nineteenth-century academic conventions. He objected indignantly however to being included among the originators of an architecture he heartily disliked.

He was unable to understand, as he made very clear, how it could be said that buildings so foreign to his in their technique and appearance, and which had discarded the traditional – the individual – craftsmanship on which he placed such value, could be linked with his buildings in any way. I suspect that those of his colleagues whom we also class among the pioneers and who were still alive in 1938 – Ashbee, Mackmurdo and Baillie Scott for example – would have said the same. And yet there *was* a link. There was a revolutionary element in their work that changed the course of English domestic architecture and afterwards, through the agency of Hermann Muthesius, of much of Europe as well.

For this reason alone an analysis of the houses Voysey designed (in chronological order so as to illustrate their evolution) such as Dr Simpson has undertaken, is invaluable; also of his furniture which, being based on structure, can be regarded as an extension of the architecture. His patterns are different. They have splendid qualities of invention and control, but I am sure Dr Simpson is right in according them a secondary place. He defines clearly the essential qualities of Voysey's architecture – more revolutionary in its time than the suburban acres of imitations make it easy for us to recognize today – and here I will only emphasize two of them: simplicity of geometrical form and insistence on reasonableness and utility. These are among the key constituents of his break-away from the conventions of his time, and these alone assure him his place in history. Besides rejecting architectural judgements based on stylistic and scholarly criteria Voysey, like Philip Webb and the early Norman Shaw, no longer looked towards monumental and aristocratic precedents (nor, more significant, to the plan-forms that went with them) but to the unselfconscious vernacular buildings of the countryside.

Dr Simpson's emphasis on Voysey's eye for geometrical form, his craftsmanlike understanding of local materials and his insistence on the unity to be gained from care for every smallest detail are an admirable basis for the appreciation of his significance for us today.

Acknowledgements

It is not possible to produce a volume of this kind without a great deal of help. I would like to thank the many owners of Voysey houses and other items for the enormous consideration they have shown at all times. The knowledge which is readily available concerning Voysey has been opened up over many years by the work of Mr John Brandon-Jones and the task of preparing this book has been made much easier by the availability of the catalogue of the collection of Voysey drawings held at the British Architectural Library, which have been comprehensively catalogued by Joanna Symonds. I am immensely grateful to both of these people. The recent exhibition of Voysey's work which was held at the Royal Pavilion, Art Gallery and Museums, Brighton and then shown at Darmstadt, Wolverhampton and Glasgow gave me the chance to carry out, in the course of organizing it, much of the background work for this book. I am grateful in particular to the Director of the Royal Pavilion, Mr John Morley, for this opportunity and for the use of many photographs which were taken for this exhibition. A book of this kind rests very heavily on the quality of illustration; the modern photographs contained in it are mostly the work of Mr Duncan MacNeill and are, as is all his work, of a high standard. I am grateful also to Mr John Barrow for supplying prints of many of the photographs used. Mr John Harris and the staff of the British Architectural Library have been, as they always are, consistently kind and helpful in responding to the many demands made upon them. To these people and so many others who have helped in various ways I offer my thanks. I also thank Sir James Richards for contributing a preface – it is an honour to have his comments included in the book.

Notes to the illustrations

Photographs reproduced are modern unless otherwise stated.

Dates given are the date of design, not of completion, unless otherwise stated.

Most drawings reproduced are in pencil on paper though occasionally ink on linen or other variants are used. Most also have a watercolour wash. The architectural drawings are referred to as 'watercolour' where there is full colouring of the elevations or perspectives. They are not necessarily in Voysey's own hand.

No attempt has been made to give full scholarly details for designs and drawings reproduced here. These are available if required in two recent publications, the RIBA Catalogue and the catalogue of the Voysey exhibition at Brighton (see Bibliography).

Introduction

Reputation is a very elusive commodity; in the contemporary architectural press and world Charles Francis Annesley Voysey was treated with massive respect which lasted for a large part of his life, culminating in the award of the Gold Medal of the RIBA in 1940, when he was an old man. He never produced a building which was not modest in size and in his career only produced about fifty in all – no great achievement for a man who, when he died in 1941, was 83. It is true that he never sought wealth and reputation; perhaps true also that he fully understood that by the attitude he took towards his work and his clients he was destroying his chances of worldly success. Yet his name is known by many who know very little about architecture and among a distinguished group of contemporary architects including Lutyens, Baillie Scott, Lethaby, Newton and others, only Lutyens is better known. Even Lutyens with his enormous reputation, competence and output lacks the cachet which Voysey's austere single-mindedness, purism and talent have given him and which have made him a keystone in the happenings in the world of architecture and design for the two decades surrounding the turn of the century. Students increasingly regard Voysey as a man whose work contains the key to what was happening in that world in the crucial years when the Victorian age was dying along with its Queen and the Edwardian taking over from it. Voysey linked himself, in his ideas and his aims, with Pugin; his critics have subsequently linked his work with the first stirrings of the Modern Movement. His two-dimensional designs are ranked along with those of William Morris. It is the basis of this reputation that this book aims to examine.

First an apology; there is very little in the following pages about Voysey's pattern design and this scant treatment might be thought strange with a man so well known for this work. There is an excuse for this and a reason. The excuse is that space is limited and only allows of an adequate dealing with three-dimensional design – architecture, furniture and allied things. The reason is that there is a wide and understandable gulf between Voysey's work in two and three dimensions; it is symptomatic that he never upholstered a furniture design with one of his own, or anyone else's, patterned fabrics. Nor did he, except very rarely, use in one of his houses a patterned covering or patterned hanging. He states that he regards patterning in this context largely as a means of hiding design defects and it was not in his nature to allow that a piece of his own design work would ever need such plastic surgery. It is therefore quite possible to consider Voysey the architect and designer and only take a sidelong look at Voysey the pattern maker.

His contribution to pattern design is considerable but needs examination elsewhere. The architectural and other work that is considered is dealt with chronologically, this despite its defects being the most comprehensible approach to use.

Fortunately the bulk of Voysey's drawings, for buildings, furniture and pattern, survive; moreover most survive in one location, the British Architectural Library to which they were recently donated by Voysey's son. Here they have been excellently catalogued and their care is now assured. There is a substantial holding also in the Print Room of the Victoria and Albert Museum. Only a few drawings are known to be still in private hands. The buildings themselves are also now sufficiently known and respected to be, in most cases, safe from threat of demolition or excessive alteration. Only one Voysey house, Gordondene at Wandsworth, is known to have been demolished and that some years ago. Only one, also, seems to have remained in the hands of the family for which it was first constructed – the other house at Wandsworth, White Cottage in Lyford Road. For this reason and because the changing taste of the 1930s found Voysey's furniture unappealing and uncomfortable, no furnished interior remains though most of the extant houses still have their original fittings in situ. Panelling, staircases, woodwork, doors and all metal fittings seem to have survived remarkably intact in almost all cases. It is refreshing, on entering many of the houses, to find the original locks and distinctive keys designed by Voysey still in use; one visitor commented that this was in itself a tribute to the feeling of integrity, completeness and comfort which is one of the strongest qualities of Voysey's domestic design and which had encouraged successive owners to keep their homes intact. Strange things have of course happened; one house is known to have had its main rooms remodelled in the style of Adam which makes a wry comment on the progress of architectural history and popular taste. To balance that it is heartening to know that one of Voysey's finest houses, Moor Crag on the shores of Windermere, has been bought by an architect whose aim is not simply to retain the fine original condition of the house but to restore the landscaping of the extensive garden, laid out by Mawson, to its original form. Another fine house on Windermere, Broadleys, is now the home of the Racing and Motor Boat Club and houses relics of the record-breaking attempts on the lake of the Campbells, father and son. Whether the strange house which Voysey designed and which was built at Aswan in Egypt still stands is not known; perhaps some traveller, better funded than the author, might care to investigate.

Voysey's furniture has had less luck. One family, the Ward Higgs, still retains a substantial number of the pieces originally commissioned for them, including some of the finest examples of his work. The Victoria and Albert Museum, the Geffrye Museum in East London, the Art Gallery and Museum in Brighton, the Whitworth Art Gallery in Manchester and the Cecil Higgins Art Gallery in Bedford all have a number of pieces which give a clear idea of the range of the furniture. Other pieces survive in private ownership but a great number which were known to have been made are now lost. It is one of the premises of this book that more attention needs to be paid to Voysey's furniture than has been in the past. Not only is the use he made of his furniture designs in composite interiors worth studying; the individual pieces are also fascinating. Considerable space will therefore be given to this aspect in the following chapters.

The title of this book stresses the point that Voysey was a man of definite, often idiosyncratic ideas to which he held strongly and consistently; his most substantial piece of writing, published in 1915, had the simple title, *Individuality*. The idea of individuality in thought and action ran perpetually through his mind just as it must force itself on those who study his work. Even so one must keep in mind a clear distinction between the idea of individuality and that of isolation. So far as one can judge at several removes, based on the accounts of remaining members of his family and of friends and acquaintances, he was a man capable of great warmth and with a high regard for the importance of friendship. Evidence – unfortunately scant concerning his private life – does bear out this fact and of course this characteristic had its impact on his professional life. Though he never worked with others, though he seems to have shunned the busy social life which his skills and reputation could have gained him, it would be wrong to think of Voysey as a man unaware of things happening around him in the fields of architecture and design. The signed menu card of a dinner held in Voysey's honour in 1927 demonstrates, by its inclusion of most of the significant names of the period in his profession, that his circle of acquaintances and friends was distinguished. This is an important distinction to make before going further; he may have kept his head often in the clouds but never in the sand.

Biographical details

1857	May 28 Born at Hessle, nr Hull: Eldest son of Rev. Charles Voysey.
1871	Family moved to Dulwich when father was deprived of living in Healaugh, Yorkshire for unorthodox preaching.
1872	Entered Dulwich College: remained there eighteen months and was afterwards educated by private tutor.
1873	Articled to J.P.Seddon for five years: remained with Seddon for a further year.
1879	Assistant to Saxon Snell for a brief period.
1880–1	Assistant to George Devey.
1881 or early 1882	Set up his own practice at Broadway Chambers, Westminster, working at small alterations and surveys.
1883	Through A.H.Mackmurdo, began work on pattern design, selling his first work to Jeffrey and Co.
1884	Joined Art Workers' Guild.
1885	Married Mary Maria Evans, living initially at 7 Blandford Road, Bedford Park, then at 45 Tierney Road, Streatham Hill, where his studio was also.
1888–9	First house built, The Cottage, Bishop's Itchington, Warwick, for M.H.Lakin.
1890–1	Moved house and studio to 11 Melina Place, St John's Wood.
1895	Moved house and studio to 6 Carlton Hill, St John's Wood.
1899	Started to build The Orchard, Chorleywood, for himself: set up a separate studio at 23 York Place, Baker Street. (The Orchard was not completed until 1900; in the meantime the family lived in a rented house nearby.)
1913	Moved studio temporarily to 25 Dover Street, then to 10 New Square, Lincolns Inn.
1917	Took flat at 73 St James's Street and lived and worked there until his death.
1924	Master of the Art Workers' Guild.
1931	Retrospective exhibition of his work held at the Batsford Gallery, London, under the auspices of the *Architectural Review*.
1936	Awarded the distinction of Designer for Industry by the Royal Society of Arts.
1940	Awarded the Royal Gold Medal of the Royal Institute of British Architects.
1941	February 12 Died at Winchester.

Chapter 1 C.F.A.Voysey:An Architect of Individuality

Biographical detail of Charles Francis Annesley Voysey's life is skimpy; there are no primary sources, no detailed diaries, not even any retrospective autobiographical account. The sources for this brief account are principally the published details given by Mr John Brandon-Jones;[1] secondly, additional details and anecdotes supplied by members of the Voysey family and others who knew him personally.

Voysey was born in 1857; at the beginning his life was unorthodox and in view of the dominant events of his early life that word is particularly apposite. He was born at Hessle, near Hull and the family soon moved to Healaugh in Yorkshire, a parish of which his father was vicar. The family numbered six children of whom Voysey was the eldest boy, kept firmly in check, we understand, by two elder sisters. The rural, even wild, environment at Healaugh would have provided Voysey, in his first fourteen years, with a strong sense of English vernacular domestic architecture. In 1871 a complete and startling change happened in the family circumstances: Voysey's father was deprived of his living and expelled from the Church of England. The details of this expulsion are not relevant except in the picture they give us of the father as a strong-minded man following his own convictions to extraordinary lengths and a man of unorthodox thinking, both in the religious sense and in a broader context. The outcome was that in his early teens Voysey found himself in the totally different environment of Dulwich in South London. Whether unsettled by this momentous family event or, more likely, as unyielding to unwelcome circumstance as his father, he rejected one aspect of the change; after a spell at Dulwich College Voysey was withdrawn and put under a private tutor. The College can supply no information on Voysey's progress while a pupil there or the specific reasons for his leaving. There had been no school at Healaugh; this absence of conventional education might account for Voysey's erratic spelling, evident in the captioning of his drawings and in those few manuscripts which survive. More important, it might account for a narrowness in his thinking, a lack of flexibility, to which his writings testify. From private tutorship Voysey moved directly to apprenticeship to J.P.Seddon, to whom he became an articled pupil in 1874. There was an architectural tradition in the family through the grandfather, Annesley Voysey; this may have influenced the choice of profession and facilitated the entry to a distinguished practice where Voysey remained articled for five years, then as assistant for a short spell.

After another short spell in the office of Saxon Snell Voysey closed this phase of his life by working for about two years in the office of George Devey. By 1882 he was working on his own and for himself. His time with Seddon and with Devey was undoubtedly important in his evolution as a designer. Yet the temptation in thinking of his career is to say that it was what he forgot when he left the tutelage of these men rather than what he learned from them that is most important. History lends a kind hand here since we actually know only fragments of the development Voysey underwent in the years between 1874 and 1882; the very few drawings that do survive from that time tell us little. Certainly he did not emerge with his future style ready formulated and the first years of his own architectural practice must have been difficult from two points of view. He had, in his own terms, much to learn before the style we think of as typical Voysey even began to emerge. While it was emerging few jobs came his way. So he was struggling to develop and struggling also to pay his way. John Brandon-Jones tells us:[2]

> It was not for several years that his practice grew large enough to occupy his full time, but he refused his father's offer to write to friends and wellwishers on his behalf. Voysey felt that a client should choose his architect because he had a liking for the man and his work, and that the advice of an architect so chosen would be more readily accepted than the advice of an architect chosen to favour a friend, or as an act of patronage.

This represented the highest of ideals; since Voysey was in his personal tastes a frugal man and also a bachelor then life probably was not too hard. By 1884, though, he was engaged and in 1885 married.

His wife can be only a shadowy figure in any account. She seems to have wielded no discernible influence on Voysey's professional life and architectural development. There are no anecdotes or accounts to cast a light on her personality or character. What the Voyseys' social life was one can only guess. Yet it does seem likely that the beginning of their relationship propelled Voysey along a course that contributed substantially, in the end, towards the forming of his overall reputation. Voysey had an acknowledged respect for the work of Arthur Heygate Mackmurdo and there grew up a substantial friendship between the two. Mackmurdo was a few years Voysey's senior, having been born in 1851; this few years' difference meant that while Voysey was still struggling to find a foothold his friend was becoming established. So it is quite plausible to accept, as Brandon-Jones suggests,[3] that Mackmurdo gave Voysey substantial help in establishing a trade in pattern designs for wallpapers and textiles. It was in 1883 that Voysey sold his first design to Jeffrey and Co.; it was therefore probably in that year – the year of Mackmurdo's famous design for the binding of *Wren's City Churches* – that this particular relationship between them was set up. It was also in this year that Voysey met Mary Maria Evans, his future wife. With his thoughts tending towards marriage and the responsibilities which for a man of his serious temperament that would entail it is not surprising that he looked to a means of livelihood which had so readily presented itself. He had a great facility with pattern, a subtle eye for colour. A pattern was a self-contained thing which did not require one to work for months in the presence of a prosperous and possibly difficult client with fixed ideas as to how he would like his new house to look. The manufacturers, attuned to the idea of the 'Morris' fabric or paper, would soon be gearing up for the new 'Art Nouveau' so it was a good time to break into the business. In the event Voysey's success in this field must have surprised him as well as pleasing him enormously and the income which he received from this side of his activities was to provide a steady income throughout his life. Some of the friendships and relationships which he set up as a result of this work were also to have impacts elsewhere; work for Essex and Co., for instance, gave him not only some of his steadiest commissions for patterns but also the friendship with Richard Walter Essex and resultant architectural commissions. He also came into prolonged contact with the Morton family which produced, as well as high-quality textiles and carpets, several personalities whom Voysey must have found stimulating; that story, though, is better told elsewhere.[4]

If Voysey's contact with the world of pattern design did come about in this way then the uneasy way in which his work sits next to his three-dimensional design is easier to accept. If anyone doubts that this uneasiness does exist then we should let Voysey speak for himself:

> A wallpaper is of course only a background and were your furniture
> good in form and colour a very simple or quite undecorated treatment
> of the walls would be preferable; but as most modern furniture is
> vulgar or bad in every way, elaborate papers of many colours help to
> disguise its ugliness. Although elaboration makes confusion more
> confounded, yet if you have but enough confusion the ugliness of
> modern life becomes bearable.[5]

This view was expressed in 1893 when Voysey was established as a designer of flat pattern, not yet fully established as an architect. It is not the intention in this chapter to go beyond outline and into detail, yet it needs to be stressed that, though he was a natural and inventive pattern designer, Voysey believed that the use of elaborate and colourful pattern in domestic settings was usually misguided. Regardless of this, the important biographical fact is that from the date of his marriage Voysey had at his disposal a means of income which drew on some of his major talents, helped to build him a reputation and brought him into contact with the sort of people who were in a position to advance his progress into a genuine architectural career. That this was his main wish there seems no cause to doubt.

By the middle of the 1890s Voysey found himself with quite as much architectural work as he could handle and the majority of his total output and of his best work was then carried out in little more than a dozen years. By the outbreak of the Great War his practice was in decline; from then on, though he lived to be an old man of eighty-three, dying in 1941, he worked relatively little. This last quarter century of his life, the start of which is conveniently signalled by the publication of his *Individuality* in 1915, has its own specific interest to the student of Voysey.

This interest will be examined in the relevant chapter; in biographical terms there is very little to note in these later years. Voysey spent them, from 1917, in a flat at 73 St James's Street. In these years he again lived alone and, also as in his early years of practice, he worked from his home. From the day the Voysey family arrived in Dulwich he seems to have had no lasting desire to leave London. His first years of practice were spent in Broadway Chambers, near the present site of New Scotland Yard in Westminster. After three years here his marriage in 1885 led to a move to Streatham Hill where he lived at 45 Tierney Road until 1890. The family then moved from South to North London, to Melina Place, St John's Wood until 1895, then to another St John's Wood address, 6 Carlton Hill, until 1899. Here the pattern was broken as the family moved to a house designed by Voysey himself, The Orchard, which was built at Chorleywood just outside London. This also meant that he could no longer work so conveniently from home as he had so far done so he set up a separate studio, initially at 23 York Place off Baker Street where he worked until 1913. Then followed a few months at 25 Dover Street and four years at 10 New Square, Lincoln's Inn. Finally, in 1917, he moved himself and his diminished practice into 73 St James's Street where he lived and worked until his death in 1941.

That there is so little biographical material available does combine with a great sense of privacy throughout his life, on Voysey's part, to leave us without a very clear idea of the sort of person he was, his personality, his interests and patterns of life. These matter little for a consideration of his work so this is no great loss. Indeed since there is a strong temptation to use personal information as a basis for interpreting the principles of an artist's work it might be a positive gain that we know so little of Voysey. We have to judge him by his work. But if for no other reason it is intriguing to know a little of the personality that stood behind the work so there can be no harm, having very briefly sketched the uneventful shape of Voysey's life, if we dwell for a few paragraphs on the character of the exceptional man who led this apparently unexceptional life.

Two contrasting sides appear in Voysey's personality; first is almost the stereotype of the strict, high-principled purist; severe, often difficult to deal with, yet undeniably and above all honourable and honest; a character containing a good deal of the puritan or the Quaker:

> ... an elderly gentleman with features greatly distinguished by the cut of his nose and the arch of his brow, the extraordinary sensitiveness and pugnacity of his mouth, and the distant, dreaming look of the visionary in his eye. Probably the first thing you would have noticed was the narrow, immaculately clean starched collar, the colour of which was the brightest thing in the room ... He was the sort of man you would never dream of taking any liberty with. You would probably have hesitated to introduce yourself. Automatically he commanded your respect.[6]

Yet on the other hand:

> Of all his remarkable attributes, the most remarkable thing about him, I think, was his smile. It was a lovely smile. There was more kindness and more simple delight in humour and more sheer affection in that smile than in any smile I have ever beheld.[6]

These comments are the views of the actor Robert Donat who some years before Voysey's death married Ella Voysey, his niece and the daughter of his favoured youngest brother Ellison. Voysey designed various things for the young couple, of whom he was obviously fond; these included some furniture, perhaps the last he ever designed, which was made and survives (see 72); and a house in Hampstead which was not built. Robert Donat's few paragraphs on 'Uncle Charles' were written and delivered as an obituary on radio and subsequently published in the *Architects Journal*. They are the closest thing we have to a subjective description of Voysey written by somebody who knew him well, liked and admired him and had the power of evocative writing. It is therefore an important though very sketchy record. It is supported by the only other source of first-hand information from people who knew him well, the comments of surviving members of the family. These bear out the point that Voysey was a man of great strength of will and stringency in his professional dealings; yet in his personal dealings capable of great warmth and kindness.

While this is not a stunning conclusion it does help to make sense of someone whose work on the one hand showed an austerity of white or plain oak surface and a lack of elaboration of detail in an age which tended towards the worship of complexity in design; yet on the other hand included designs for soft and delicately coloured patterns, the principal images of which were bird, leaf, flower and fruit. To this picture of an austere but warm kindness we only need to add the notion of a sense of humour to capture the basic qualities. Even when expressing the most severe and puritanical of his ideas Voysey sometimes slipped, easily enough to make it seem quite natural, into a dry humour. It was his obsession that all objects surrounding him, even down to the smallest, should be the epitome of their type. This was a lofty enough ideal and one which most of us would find finicky and off-putting, even from as respectable a source as Mr Voysey. Yet somehow we can go along with it when he puts it in this way:

Cold vegetables are less harmful than ugly dish covers. One affects the body and the other affects the soul.[7]

Particularly since we also have the account of a family member who recalls that the same man could be taken to eat in a restaurant and comment as he sat: 'I may not be hungry but, thank the Lord, I am greedy'.

Finally in this introductory chapter it is vital to add a reminder. Very few people, designers or others, have been fortunate and talented enough to stand completely distinct from their generation when their work is considered. To claim that Voysey was such a person would be extravagant; in any case our judgement of this would be highly subjective. Many people might agree with the author that there is indeed something quite distinctive about going into a Voysey house and that the only other architects of that generation to equal that distinctiveness are Mackintosh and Lutyens. That judgement is very open to accusations of modishness, of fashion-following, particularly now when Art Nouveau is much in evidence on the coffee table and in the Portobello Road. But at the least most people would agree that, like it or not, there is a distinct newness or difference about a Voysey house in its time and context. That is the necessary reminder: it may look to us now like a better-conceived element of suburbia but a Voysey house, in its day, had a complete freshness about it. It is in the essence of that freshness that it has subsequently been copied and in the copying lost. It is important to let the feeling of freshness work on us when we look at Voysey. This feeling is one that was picked out by Sir Edwin Lutyens in 1931, when Voysey's reputation was just starting to revive after some years of neglect:

> No detail was too small for Voysey's volatile brain, and it was not so
> much his originality – though original he was – as his consistency
> which proved a source of such delight. Simple, old-world forms
> moulded to his own passion, as if an old testament had been rewrit in
> vivid print, bringing to light a renewed vision in the turning of its
> pages, an old world made new and with it, to younger men, of whom I
> was one, the promise of a more exhilarating sphere of invention. This
> was Voysey's achievement – Fashions, as they ever have and ever will
> do, come and go. Hail! then to those men amongst whom Voysey
> stands, who give new kindling to the old flames to warm and cheer
> conviction in a living future.[8]

It was echoed ten years later, by J.M.Richards, in his obituary notice on Voysey's
death:

> Into this stuffy atmosphere blew a breath of fresh air . . . It is difficult for
> us today to appreciate the extent to which Voysey was a revolutionary,
> for we are surrounded by the indirect descendants of his small houses,
> debased almost beyond recognition but yet representing, however
> inadequately, a way of living infinitely more humane than the way he
> helped to break away from.[9]

Chapter 2 Establishing a Practice – The Years up to 1895

The establishment of a substantial architectural practice was a laborious business for Voysey; he did not make it easier for himself since, as John Brandon-Jones tells us in his *Memoir*, he refused the help of his father in encouraging friends to patronize the young architect. Until 1890 business was very slow but from then, with Walnut Tree Farm, near Malvern (1890) and the Bedford Park house (1891), more substantial commissions began to come in. The *Studio* of September 1893 carried a substantial interview with 'Mr Charles F. Annesley Voysey, Architect and Designer'[1] and, while it was a considerable achievement to have won this recognition, the emphasis is heavily on pattern design work. When, towards the end of the piece, the subject of architectural designs is introduced it is done in a way which lacks conviction: 'It is not fair to regard Mr Voysey as a designer alone . . .' – though this is manifestly what the piece has done. By June 1897, however, it is a different matter: a whole article is devoted to the work of Voysey as a component of 'The Revival of English Domestic Architecture' and this article deals in some detail with most of the works of the early years of his practice.[2]

In 1888 the *Architect* published a design for a cottage by Voysey the address on which – 7 Blandford Road, Bedford Park – dates it to the very few months after his marriage in 1885 which he spent at this address. This design is in no way surprising viewed as the work of a young architect in the mid 1880s; yet it was taken up, republished in the *Studio* in a slightly reworked form in 1894 as an 'Artist's Cottage', and is invariably cited in discussions of Voysey's work (1). It has a few of the Voysey trademarks – horizontal strips of leaded windows, those at first-floor level tucked up under the eaves; the eaves themselves having a deep overhang, the gutter supported on smoothly curved metal brackets; the walls having shallow buttresses and, apparently, a roughcast render. Less typically it is fashionably half-timbered, a practice which Voysey speedily dropped; and the layout is idiosyncratic, a spacious 28ft × 14ft 6in. 'living and work room' absorbing so much space that the 'picture gallery and lounge' behind is over 20ft long but only 6ft deep. On the rear elevation, except for a squat corner tower, the roof sweeps down close to ground-floor level, truncating the available bedroom space to good visual effect but to no real purpose. Possibly as a result of the publication of this design Voysey was commissioned by M.H. Lakin to design a cottage to be built at Bishop's Itchington; this he did and the house was built (2). The half-timbering was dropped though initially Lakin had considered it as a possibility; the buttressing and partially jettied first floor, which can be seen again

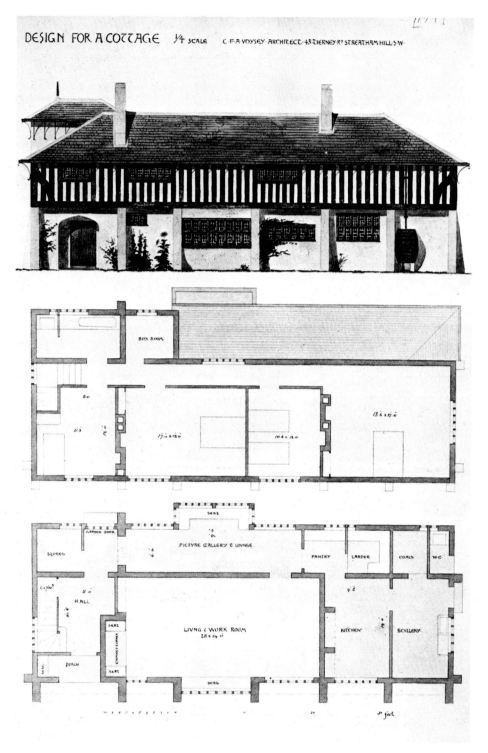

DESIGN FOR A COTTAGE ¼ SCALE   C·F·A·VOYSEY·ARCHITECT·45 TIERNEY R? STREATHAM HILL·S·W·

1
Design for a cottage, probably designed in a
form similar to this in 1885; published as here
1888. Unexecuted. Elevation and plans.

2
The Cottage at Bishop's Itchington, near
Warwick, for M.H.Lakin, 1888.

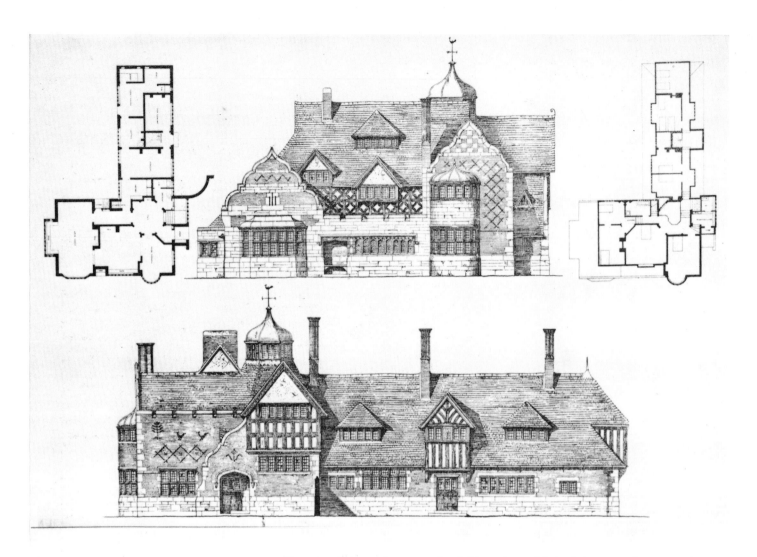

3
Design for a house having an octagonal hall, published in the *British Architect*, 1889. Unexecuted. Elevations and plans.

at Perrycroft (see 14), are retained from the published design. There is a pleasing porch and lean-to with strip windows each having a hipped, tiled roof. Less pleasing is the slight raising into the eaves of several of the upper windows, covered with barely projecting hipped dormers which produce a hesitant series of breaks in the sweep of the roof. These two projects, the design and the cottage, are an uneasy balance of emphatic features and detailing set against self-conscious mannerisms.

Three other designs, all for unexecuted projects, also survive from this pre-1890 period and throw light on Voysey's activities then. Two were published in the *British Architect* in 1889,[3] though probably dating from two or three years earlier. The design for a house with an octagonal hall (3) is probably the earlier, owing as it does a great deal to the influence of Voysey's masters and the generally used stylistic devices of the period. It is an èclectic and very cheerful design, having

4
Design for a house, published in the *British Architect*, 1889 and known, from its attenuated form, as a tower house. Unexecuted. Front elevation and plans.

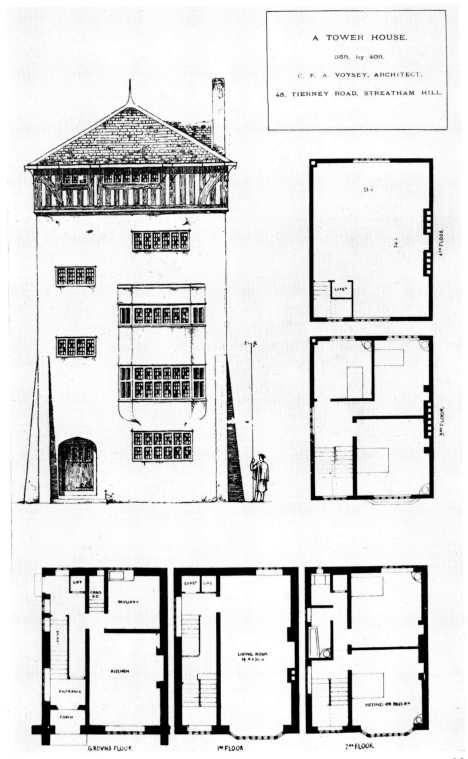

A TOWER HOUSE.

38ft. by 40ft.

C. F. A. VOYSEY, ARCHITECT.

48, TIERNEY ROAD, STREATHAM HILL.

GROUND FLOOR   1ST FLOOR   2ND FLOOR

5
First design for a house at Bedford Park in
Chiswick for Mrs Forster, 1888. Not executed
in this form. Front elevation.

PROPOSED HOVSE FOR MRS FORSTER
AT BEDFORD PARK. CHISWICK
1/4" SCALE

FRONT ELEVATION.

C.F.A. VOYSEY. ARCH
45 BIERNEY ROAD
STREATHAM HILL S.W
AVG 19 1888.

decorative brickwork, figures and devices freely used alongside stone walls, crenellations, timber-frame and Dutch gables, decorative half-timbering, gabled and hipped dormers, bow windows, stone mullioned and transomed window frames and the ogee curve of the roof lantern and the roofing over the bows. Perhaps young Voysey was trying to get all the decorative complexity which this building incorporates out of his system in one go. The resultant heterogeneity is very well handled, markedly lacking the unease which, as suggested above, then crept into the designs of the next few years. The 'Tower House' of the mid- or late-1880s is a complete contrast (4); its severe form and fenestration – emphasized by the two small between-floors staircase windows – is relieved only by the angle-buttresses, the oriel window, the quite bizarre fourth-floor half-timbering and the arched opening to the porch. Its main eccentricity is excused, presumably, since it is the result of a brief to produce a lot of living space on a narrow site. The Tower House here shown has the charm of an ungainly, gangling puppy, but might not be much fun to live either in or next to. If the open fourth floor were intended to be a studio or workroom then, with its restricted window openings, tucked up below the overhanging eaves, it would not be a joy to work in either. The third of these early, unexecuted projects is different in that it was the result of a brief from a client, a Mrs Forster who wanted a house built at Bedford Park. The problem was to fit a new building into the completed ranges of homes in Bedford Park which represented an avant-garde development of the previous decade; Voysey's initial answer to it, designed in 1888 (5) makes some concession to the setting and also shows a debt to his training. Only the upper part is rendered and the bay window of conventional form; the window layout shows clear signs of Voysey's developing distinctiveness, the gutter brackets are beginning to look familiar and we even see what looks to be a prototype of the long cast-iron strap hinge terminating in a heart shape at the top of the entrance door. These hinges are endemic in Voysey's later work. This design certainly does not have the distinctiveness of either of the other two designs noted above; possibly the nearness of an actual client unnerved Voysey; presumably the design he produced unnerved the client as well for when the Bedford Park house was finally built three years later the final design (see 5) was much closer in spirit to the idiosyncratic Tower House than to this first draft.

It will be apparent by now that there is not a tremendous amount of evidence on which to judge these early years; yet there is no reason to think that Voysey worked on more projects than have survived. There is no executed building before the very end of the 1880s; there is no reason to think that the few projects which are known are the survivors from a culling in later years by their author. If he had weeded out his early designs on some retrospective basis in his mature years there is no rationale obvious now which could tell us why he preserved these particular designs. So we can conclude that we have the substantial part of the architectural work of the early years at our disposal. It is a very fair selection; original, inventive, but too concerned with manner and with stylistic trickery.

After these various projects and the one house at Bishop's Itchington work suddenly began in earnest. In the first two years of the 1890s there were four projects all being built: the Bedford Park house was taken up again and redesigned; there was a studio in West Kensington; two town houses in a terrace in Knightsbridge; a substantial farm house near Malvern. It is difficult to sort out the exact chronology of these projects and since they were so close together in date it seems permissible to deal with them in the most convenient way from a critical point of view. The house at 14 South Parade, Bedford Park, for the Forsters, is a very workable compromise between two previous projects, the first design for the site of 1888 and the Tower House, both described above. The front elevation, idiosyncratically tall and slender and with a low pitched roof, resembles the Tower House with its ground-floor storey cut away (6). It has a deeper, square bay, terminating in a canopy with concave curves which has Georgian overtones. This deep bay and the new entrance position, now moved round to the side, minimize the drawbacks of the narrow frontage. Nevertheless accommodation space is cramped since the whole second floor is given over to a studio room lit principally by a rear-facing window, almost of full width, which carries up into the roofline. The significance of this design as executed is that it loses the obvious drawbacks of the two parent designs: the uneasy domestic character of Voysey's first design for the house, which represented a hangover from the days of his training, is gone; so also is the ungainly half-timbering which marred the severity of the Tower House design. The deficiencies in living space in this house were soon acknowledged by the addition in 1894 of a side extension on two floors. The disruption this has caused to the original effect is apparent at first glance and does reflect on the impracticality of Voysey's first efforts here. Even so the house is a striking one, effective even now and impressive as the first substantial contribution of its designer to the architecture of his day; doubly impressive when the 'newness' of its appearance is remembered. When the house was built the inhabitants of Bedford Park thought it ill-conceived and unsuitable – but for the reason that it was 'old-fashioned' in appearance and not at all the thing for that progressive suburb. This apparent contradiction should be remembered in later discussions of Voysey's place in the progression of the vernacular style of his day. This building shows the first use of the window detailing which became a trademark of the Voysey house, employing leaded panes set in an iron frame, with iron fittings, within stone dressings. It also provides the setting for the story, the original source of which is lost but which was recorded in the *Studio*:

> It is amusing to read that it was found necessary, in order to prevent the builder from displaying the usual 'ovolo mouldings', 'stop chamfers', fillets, and the like, to prepare eighteen sheets of contract drawings to show where his beloved ornamentation *was to be omitted*. This topsy-turvy proceeding is delightfully suggestive of the entirely mechanical adornment in general use which is so thoroughly a part of the routine that great pains have to be taken to prevent the workmen from unconscious 'decoration', according to their wonted habit.[4]

The same writer also notes that the contract price of £494.10s was extremely low, 'a price that takes one's breath away'.

In strong contrast, though again intended as studio and living accommodation for an artist, is the building for W.E.F.Britten at 17 St Dunstan's Road in West

6
Perspective sketch by T.Raffles Davison of a
house at 14 South Parade, Bedford Park,
Chiswick, for Mrs Forster as executed from a
design of 1891.

An Artist's
House
CFA Voysey
Architect

Rambling Sketches 812
T Raffles Davison

Kensington (7). This is a squat, two-storey house, its lowness emphasized by the low-pitched hipped roof with a deep eaves overhang. The eaves at the front project out past the dormer window in a manner that we will see often in later houses. Other devices added to the Voysey vocabulary with this house include the tapered chimney-stack, roughcast like the walls; the deeply projecting porch cantilevered out on wooden supports (in this case further supported by a wrought-iron stay); the use of a grotesque profile, probably caricaturing the client, in this case carved into the porch supports. These devices all recur regularly in his later work. No other house, unfortunately, has the plain but elegant wrought- and cast-iron railings which ornament the front of the St Dunstan's Road house.

The last of the trio of London buildings dating from the first years of the 1890s is the pair of terraced houses, numbers 14 and 16 Hans Road in Knightsbridge, facing the west elevation of Harrods. It is strange that the writer of the *Studio* article quoted states that these two houses lack the originality of other early Voysey designs; his words are that they 'do not amaze you by sheer novelty as Mr Britten's studio surprises'. We must bow down to this contemporary assessment of the impact of these designs yet it is hard to understand. There is much of interest in these two houses, the only ones in Voysey's work where he suffered the constraints of infilling into an existing terrace. The most marked feature (after the use of brickwork rather than roughcast, which we can accept was imposed upon a reluctant Voysey by the demands of client and of setting) is the blending of line and curve in the façade. Curves are seen in the low walls flanking the entrance stairs, the upswept quadrant curve on the parapet at the party walls, the pair of small semicircular oriel windows and the moulding of the corbelling to support these and the main oriel windows. Contrasting with this are the squareness of the flat-roofed porch and the drip-mouldings over the lower windows which are carried through into decorative stone courses running the width of the houses. The severe symmetry of this pair of houses is emphasized by the angular descent of the down-pipes. The only slight flourish is the appearance of the heart shape – later so typical of Voysey – framing the house numbers on the porch. What the line drawing (8a) cannot convey, which the photograph (8b) does, is the strong sense of horizontality which Voysey's houses have compared with their neighbours in the street.

The three buildings described above show the emergence of many of the main features of Voysey's mature style, particularly when contrasted with the earlier unexecuted designs. All three, however, show Voysey dealing with a town site, an oddity for an architect whose reputation rests on the evolution of a successful style of medium-size vernacular country house. The designing of Walnut Tree Farm in open country at Castlemorton, in clear view of the Malvern Hills, has therefore a double importance as an early design for a house of substantial size and as the first significant commission for a country house (9a). Designed in 1890 it is L-shaped with the services situated in the subsidiary wing of the L; a line of stables and outbuildings close a third side and form a sort of entrance courtyard. The setting is flat country eastwards and in the lee of the Malvern Hills though the orientation of the house has the main elevation, the garden front, facing away from the hills. It is crucial to remember that the house was built to replace the old, timber-frame farmhouse which stands just north of it; contemporary photographs show this in reasonable condition such that it could be mistaken, at a distance, for part of Voysey's work; now this old house stands in a shamefully ruinous condition. The presence of a fine timber-frame building on site was almost certainly what swayed Voysey into using half-timbered detailing – which was in no way structural – and therefore we should not read Walnut Tree Farm as a serious attempt to instate timber-frame work, sham or genuine, as a component of Voysey's style. Like Bishop's Itchington this house has a jettied first floor on the garden front though this is disguised by the chimney breast, porch, polygonal window bay, and series of buttresses to read as a series of recessed bays. Above, the dormers have been given the conviction they lacked at Bishop's Itchington by the addition of gables with half-timbered detailing; the guttering is carried in front of the bedroom windows supported only by the now familiar curved brackets. The principal feature of the entrance elevation, by contrast, is the sweeping down of the pitched roof to eaves at ground-floor window level, less than head height. This considerable expanse of roof is broken only by a dormer and the projecting

SKETCHES OF LONDON STREET ARCHITECTURE.—V.
HOUSES IN HANS-ROAD. Mr. C. F. A. VOYSEY, ARCHITECT.

8a
Perspective sketch of two houses, Nos. 14 and 16 Hans Road, Knightsbridge, for Archibald Grove, 1891–2, showing the houses as executed.

8b
Nos. 14 and 16 Hans Road shown in the terrace of which they form a part. No. 12, to the right, is by Arthur Heygate Mackmurdo.

pitched roof over the porch. The most remarkable feature of this exaggerated detailing of the roof is the dramatic end elevation it produced (9b). A fine coloured perspective sketch of the garden front (9c) demonstrates that Voysey introduced here for the first time his favourite colouring scheme – a white roughcast render, woodwork of a strong mid-green and curtains uniformly throughout the house of a bright red. The plan layout shows the simplicity characteristic of Voysey's early designs as indeed of many later ones: a staircase beside the main door, a corridor running the length of the entrance front at ground- and first-floor level, a strip of rooms opening off this corridor. The only complication is the staggering of the upper floor, made necessary by the narrowing caused by the low sweep of the roof

30

9a
Walnut Tree Farm, Castlemorton, near
Malvern, for R.H.Cazalet, 1890. The garden
front as it is today.

on the entrance front; this is compensated for, and turned to stylistic advantage, by the jettying on the garden front already referred to.

Early furniture designs and other work

After this group of houses were built up to 1891, there comes a brief gap before the progression to houses at Colwall and Frensham which bring the account up to 1895. This is therefore a good point at which to consider the other ways in which Voysey's career had been expanding in these early years. The *Black Book*[5] records designs for furniture in 1889 for an A.I.Collis or Collin and for the Essex and Co. showrooms; also furniture for A.A.Voysey for a house at Higham, Kent, in 1892. None of this survives or is identifiable. For the 1880s there are two instances of furniture designs which do survive. The first is a design for a chair, known as the Swan chair because of the low-relief carved swans' heads which terminate the rear supports. A chair to this pattern was certainly made about 1896 for W.Ward Higgs and exhibited in the Arts and Crafts Exhibition of that year. The design

9b
Walnut Tree Farm, end elevation.

9c
Walnut Tree Farm, perspective watercolour from the garden with plans inset.

33

which survives, however, can be dated by watermark and by the address 'Broadway Chambers' which Voysey has inscribed on it to between 1883 and 1885. As can be seen (10) the chair has a form unlike anything else designed by Voysey. Structurally it is simple – flat section oak, the side members interlocked in an X-shape, the joints all pegged or dowelled. But the flat side members are cut to free curves and the ends carved to bird's head form. The chair has strong links with the English vernacular which relate both to the influences of Voysey's training and to his inclination to think in terms of the past. Perhaps in the Swan chair there is an influence from Pugin, who was one of Voysey's heroes; certainly there is about it a feeling of the early seventeenth century. Very similar in its roots, though as different as can be in the nature of its outward appearance, is the design for a table of 1888 (11). It also is oak, the native British timber which Voysey used almost without exception for his furniture. It has – again a precedent for most of his later furniture – a plain finish, in this case 'to be fumigated, not to be polished'. The timber is heavy, square sectioned, unrelieved by any decoration; only the segmental drop leaves relieve with their curve the simple solidity. More sophisticated but falling into a laboured, cottage style is the cabinet of 1893 designed for Lady Wentworth (12). Here the style of Voysey's later furniture can be seen developing, the plain oak surfaces, deeply projecting but simple mouldings, carefully considered proportions and a craftsmanlike finish contrasting with austerity of appearance.

There is no record in these early years of an interior completely designed and fitted by Voysey; there is, for that matter, no assured knowledge of the growth of his interest in combining the design of interior fittings and detail with the design of

10
The Swan chair, designed *c.*1883–5. The seat padding is not original.

11
Design for an oak table for M.H.Lakin, 1889.

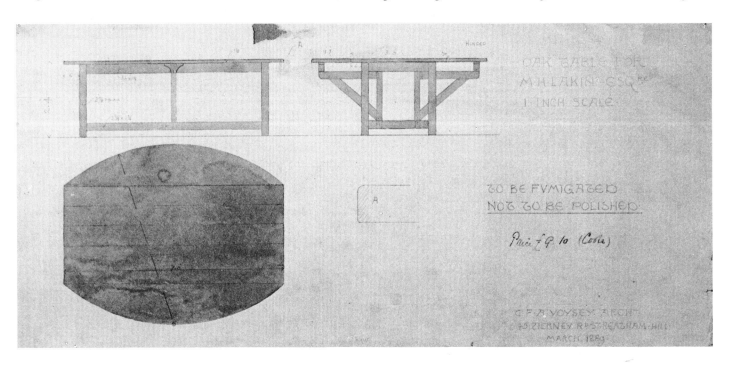

12
Cabinet for Lady Wentworth, 1893. In a
slightly modified form to that shown here, the
cabinet is illustrated in the *Studio* of May 1896,
possibly suggesting that more than one
example was made.

his buildings. There is, however, a very strong clue to the direction his thoughts
were taking in a design of 1890 which survives. This Voysey entitled 'Suggestion
for Treatment of a Domestic Window' and it is an interesting treatment. It is
ornate and loosely tudoresque; the chief features (13) are the heavy, moulded
stone mullions; the leaded glass with oval stained-glass panels set in iron casement
frames; the green stained panelled wood surrounds. It foreshadows his later work
in that all details, notably the window fittings, are distinctively to his own design.
Yet it is essentially an ornate treatment, perhaps suited to the interior of the 'House
with an Octagonal Hall', certainly not to the Bedford Park house. It is elegant but
lacks Voysey's later restraint. He had joined, in 1884, the Art Workers' Guild, and
was to become in 1924 its Master; it is clear that his interests lay for the large part of
his professional life in the design of the house and fittings entire. This interest
stemmed presumably from the early influences of Mackmurdo and others and
was, among the practitioners of the Arts and Crafts movement, a widely held one.
W.R.Lethaby wrote in 1892:

> So it matters much that such things as are about you be each of their
> kind good; carefully wrought and thoughtfully shaped – beautiful.[6]

In 1894 Voysey put forward some views on domestic furniture to the General
Meeting of the Royal Institute of British Architects, a lecture that was later
published:

Mankind is still very much in the monkey stage. We mock and mimic old and new work, good and bad . . . From one extreme to another we rock, without any sign of regaining an equilibrium.[7]

This was his first sally at revivalism and the imitation of past styles, a subject that caused him, along with so many of his colleagues and predecessors in the nineteenth century, a great deal of confused thought and indeterminate conclusion. He went on to say, on a narrower tack:

It is clear then that we must have a logical basis for our design in furniture; as in all else, laws must be discovered and obeyed.[7]

But without defining these laws for which he searched he had to go on:

I fear I am expected to say something much more practical about the

13
Design entitled, 'Suggestion for Treatment of a Domestic Window', 1890. No client is named so the design is assumed to be an unexecuted project.

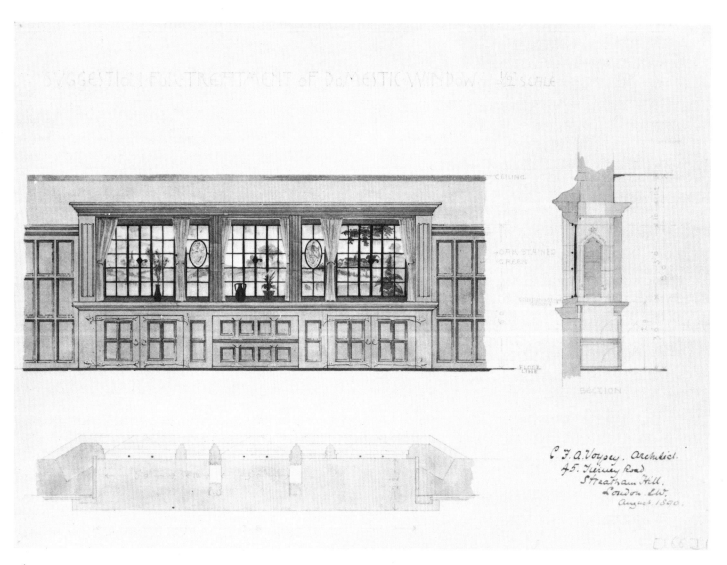

36

> design of furniture. I wish I could say something helpful but I am
> myself groping in the dark, struggling to find out the true laws which
> govern fitness and beauty.[7]

In the evidence that survives from these early years we do see a little of the struggle to which Voysey refers; we do not see enough to be clear about it. From his later years it is comforting to deduce a strong feeling of what is 'right' in architecture and its allied skills; from these early comments it is congenial for us to assume that the struggle for laws to 'discover and obey' did leave him 'groping in the dark'. What we actually see from the evidence available is a disciplining process, initially a paring away of excess detail. The interesting thing about this detail, at this stage, is that it is the detail of history or tradition, the stylistic influences of English vernacular. This is the backcloth one would have expected Voysey to begin with, working as he did from his background and training. The remarkable thing was how quickly and completely he shed the appearance of it in his work, while retaining its mood. The spirit of a vernacular style and the sense of designing buildings for a country which had a long history and in a style appropriate to that history remained with him. If that seems a nebulous or meaningless distinction one can only say that it is necessary to try to understand it for there seems no other way to reconcile the two aspects of Voysey's work: first his apparent, increasing absorption with the British native past; second the interest which the sparseness and economy of his work created among the next generation of architects, who were to do things quite foreign to his own inclinations and interests, just as most of his were foreign to theirs.

Perrycroft and Lowicks

When Voysey made the above comments to the RIBA his biggest architectural venture to date and first building to attract substantial notice was completed. This was Perrycroft which like Walnut Tree Farm was sited near Malvern. Perrycroft had from the start advantages which the earlier house lacked; it was situated outstandingly on the steep west slope of the Malvern Hills and it commanded, as well as this more than generous site, an ample budget of almost £5000 against the £1120 of Walnut Tree Farm. Did Voysey take full advantage of this chance? Initially, no. The house does not extract the full value from the site as did some of his later houses, notably Moor Crag; it stands square on an excavated terrace, commanding the best of the views. The plan is L-shaped, the service wing in the tail of the L (14a), and the two main elevations are quite different in mood, a common feature in Voysey's work. The drive comes down steeply and round into the angle of the L, the way the site is cut back into the hillside preventing a clear long-distance view of the entrance façade. The L in fact carries back a little way into a third side, creating a narrow west wing which looks out direct over the ground west of the Malvern Hills. The atmosphere of this entrance court (14b) retains something of Voysey's first projects, something of the 'House with an Octagonal Hall', in the tower and porch with their leaded roofs of complex double curves. Notable also is an unbroken run of windows at first-floor level. On the garden side – looking steeply down but not directly out to the plain to the west

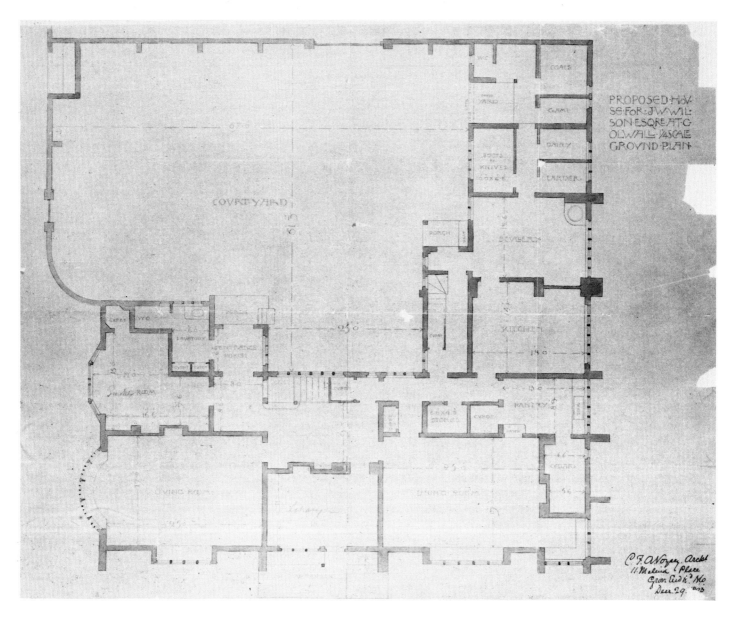

PROPOSED·HOV
SE·FOR·J·W·WIL:
SON·ESQRE·AT·C
OLWALL·¼SCALE
GROVND·PLAN

14a
Ground plan for Perrycroft at Colwall, near
Malvern, for J. W. Wilson, 1893–4.

– is a long sweep of hipped roof; on the entrance side the tower, a dormer, the
chimney-stacks all break the roofline but here it is clean. There is a slight jetty, the
timber corbels to the upstairs bays are rustic in character, the window frames are
timber not stone (14c). This and the half-timbering to the top of the tower are
concessions to the setting and the area; not much else is. The designs for Perrycroft
are dated from Dec 1893 to Jan 1894 so over three years separate it from Walnut
Tree Farm; yet although the houses are quite different in scale, Perrycroft being
bigger and more lavish, their strengths and weaknesses are much the same. Both

14b
Perrycroft, the entrance courtyard.

strive to incorporate vernacular or traditional detail with the clean, plain style which is becoming typical of Voysey. Both adopt simple layouts providing unfussy living conditions. Each house is quite well adapted for use by its inhabitants. Neither, on the other hand, – and this is the principal weakness – is particularly well reconciled to its setting, which indicates the unease which Voysey still felt in this aspect of his work.

Quite how Voysey established his link with the area around Malvern is unknown; following the building of these two substantial projects he designed an

39

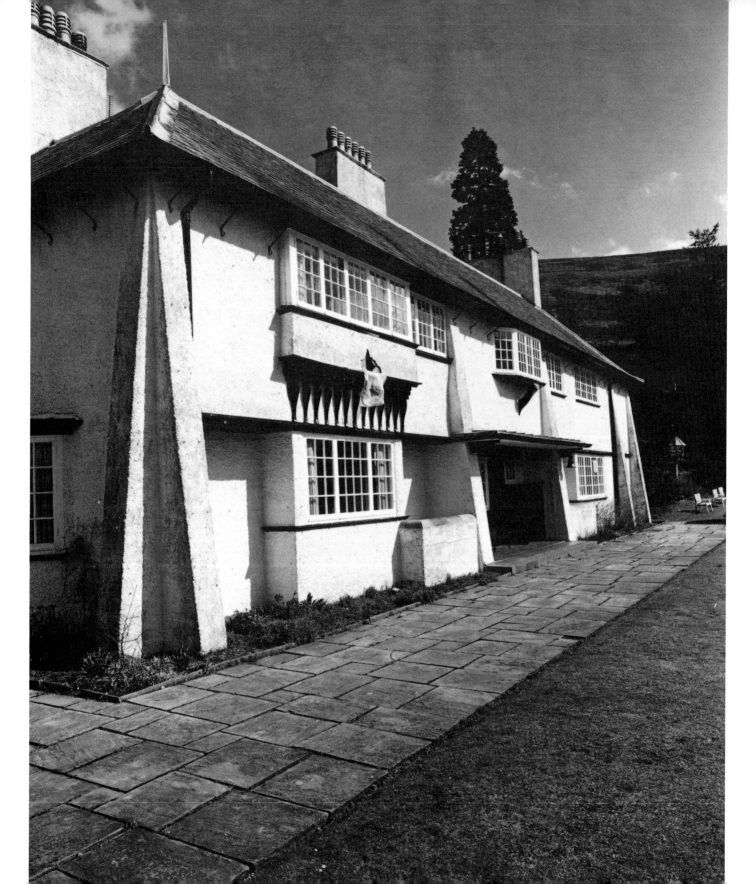

unexecuted house there for himself in 1897 so it was obviously a part of the
country which appealed to him. However the pull was not strong enough to get
him away from London. In the meantime he designed and built a house, starting in
1895, for his father in Platt's Lane, Hampstead; it was a plain L-shaped house of
low budget, reinforcing the development of the medium-sized house which was
the backbone of his practice. More excitingly a commission came in 1894 from a
client whose work was to play an important part for Voysey – his first
commission, in fact, from a substantial and established client who would be in a
position to contribute to his career. The client was E.J.Horniman of the tea family
and that he liked the work Voysey produced for him is evidenced since he came
back with more commissions which we shall consider in later chapters. This first
project was to build a house near Frensham in Surrey, the first of Voysey's several
important commissions in this part of the Home Counties. As the final item in this
opening chapter Lowicks, as the house was named, is satisfying; it helps to sum up
what has been happening and it looks forward. All the earlier houses and projects
have been idiosyncratic, which is not a bad thing, but have also been self-
conscious, which is. That is why, for instance, Perrycroft produces a slight feeling
of unease. There it sits, a substantial house in a spectacular setting which we can
rationalize as a contribution in vernacular vein to the progress of contemporary
domestic architecture and can applaud as such; yet it is awkward. Lowicks comes
right out with its stylistic awkwardness in a much more honest way, more mature.
Thus it makes a virtue of it (15). The house is compact with a single-storey service
wing; the main block, rectangular with a hipped roof, has to accommodate three

storeys, the top one being an attic room. The roof therefore sports windows recessed into the heavily overhanging eaves, a plain flat-roofed dormer and an elaborate half-timbered one with hipped, tiled roof. The house at Frensham, though not one of Voysey's finest, is the clearest and most enjoyable sign that he has grown up as an architect, has developed the confidence to do what he wants, to assert himself and to be at ease in doing so.

It is particularly appropriate therefore that it should be on Lowicks that we have a rare account, and the earliest, of what it was like to-be inside a Voysey house:

> Lowicks was equally [the writer has just been discussing another home not by Voysey] beguiling and even more idiosyncratic, partly because everything was very high or very low. The roof, for instance, came down steeply almost to the ground; the casement windows were wide and low and the window seats very low; but the latches on the doors were very high and to open them one had to make a gesture like that of proposing a toast; straight and very high were the backs of the chairs which . . . were pierced with heart-shaped openings; on high shelves near the ceiling stood vases of crafty green pottery filled with peacocks' feathers; and the hot water cans, coal-scuttles, electroliers and so on were made of beaten or hammered brass or copper. It was still, this house, the last word, or at any rate the last but one, in modern taste and comfort.[8]

What is interesting is what, at the time of visiting, fascinated the writer. The low sweep of the roof and lowness in general came first; loftiness, after all, had always been associated with grandeur or prestige so its lack would be striking. The high-backed chairs pierced with hearts — as we shall see, a typical Voysey design — strengthened the impression of lowness in the rooms. The small items of furniture, and the ornaments, all conformed to and helped to consolidate the mood of the house; overall the impression was that this was fashionable, modern and also comfortable. One cannot judge the success of Voysey as a designer solely in the context of contemporary opinion; yet it is important to be reminded constantly of the extent to which his work was considered innovatory and extraordinary.

As the last five years of the nineteenth century began Voysey found himself with a practice fast becoming established; he had good press notice including considerable mention in Europe where the Germans in particular thought well of his work. Though Voysey never cared to travel his scrap book shows that he kept a close eye on all publication of his work, in England and overseas. He had acquired a sense of confidence and accomplishment in carrying out the type of design which, he had persuaded himself and a body of clients, was practical and worthwhile. He was also about to produce a spate of furniture designs and other detail work. He was poised to become one of the leading figures in British architecture and design depending on his performance over the next few years.

Chapter 3   Some Important Experiments, 1895–7

The single most important house designed by Voysey was Moor Crag, the drawings for which are dated 1898. There were some earlier designs which were direct precursors of it and houses in later years which did not owe it a great deal. Yet if one sat down to list the qualities which go to make up the ideal Voysey house and then cast around for the house which, in its finished form, most closely approached fulfilling these qualities or requirements, Moor Crag would be the one. In speaking in this chapter of some 'important experiments' which immediately pre-date that house, this is to be borne in mind. The architectural content of this chapter covers a small group of houses, the principal two being Norney (now Norney Grange), near Shackleford, and New Place, originally called Hurtmore, in Haslemere; both were designed in 1897 with later additions. These houses were unlike anything Voysey was to design later; on the other hand both owed a good deal to some of the earlier designs, notably to Perrycroft which is discussed above. With this in mind it might seem odd to refer to them as 'experiments'. Something which sits on the basis of past work and does not lead anywhere does not seem a prime candidate to be so called. However, as indicated in the previous chapter, Voysey was coming in 1895 to a watershed. He was beginning to achieve a limited success and to be seen as some sort of promoter of an avant-garde; he was beginning also to show considerable confidence in his approach to architectural and other design problems but he had not done a great deal of work, not completed many buildings and not achieved yet a real fluency in his work. The buildings to be considered in this chapter were important in that – as will be shown – they marked his final and most important experiment with fluency in design. Without them, Moor Crag and the other mature Voysey houses could never have happened.

In this period of three years or so Voysey also began to produce the style of furniture which we now see as typical of him; between 1895 and 1898 he evolved most of the patterns of furniture which he used, both as one-off pieces and as more or less regular lines, throughout his career.

Of the projects which were under way in 1896, the year before the masterly efforts of Norney and New Place, three are notable: the house for Julian Sturgis on the Hogs Back near Guildford; the group of workmen's cottages at Elmesthorpe, outside Leicester, for the Earl of Lovelace; the studio and living accommodation for A. Sutro at Studland Bay in Dorset. They evince three very different styles.

16
Perspective watercolour and plans, inset, for a house, now called Greyfriars, on the Hog's Back near Guildford, Surrey, for Julian Sturgis, 1896–7. This watercolour, signed H.Gaye, was exhibited at the Royal Academy, 1897.

The Sturgis house has been known as Merlshanger and Wancote; today it is called Greyfriars and it is most convenient to use that name in referring to it. As seen in the elevation and plan (16) it is of the type of long, narrow house which Voysey repeated several times; here the narrowness is partly necessary since the steeply sloping site on the scarp slope falling south off the Hogs Back does not allow of much depth; equally important, this layout allows as many rooms as possible the benefit of the splendid view. This house clearly looks forward to Moor Crag, particularly in the bold sweep of the roof from the cross gable down to eaves below the top line of the ground-floor windows. The row of six cottages designed for one of Voysey's aristocratic occasional patrons, the Earl of Lovelace, for his estate outside Leicester, is one of few designs by Voysey for a terrace of housing for working-class occupancy – the development for Henry Briggs's colliery at Whitwood, Yorkshire (see 41) is the only other significant example which was built. In addition there was a proposed design for cottages for the Earl of Beauchamp for Madresfield Court, Malvern Link, of 1901, and one or two other minor schemes. The Elmesthorpe cottages are as can be seen (17) quite unextraordinary in general design and layout; their interest lies in the whimsical arrangement of the thatched roof and this is even more apparent in the proposal for thatching the Madresfield Court cottages of 1901 which are mentioned above (18). Thatch had two main attractions for Voysey; first it was a traditional and assertively vernacular material; second it had a plasticity in use which slate or tile lacked, it could curve and flow over the roof and around the windows. This is precisely the effect Voysey sought in the roofing at Elmesthorpe and even more in the proposal for Madresfield Court. The thatch flows down to cover the porch, parts and flows around the dormers. The effect is whimsical, exaggerated, romantic; above all it is superficial for when we look at the Elmesthorpe cottages

17
Design for a terrace of six thatched cottages at
Elmesthorpe, near Leicester, for the Earl of
Lovelace, 1896. Front elevation, cross-section
and ground- and first-floor plans. The cottages
were executed and still stand, although with
slated roofs.

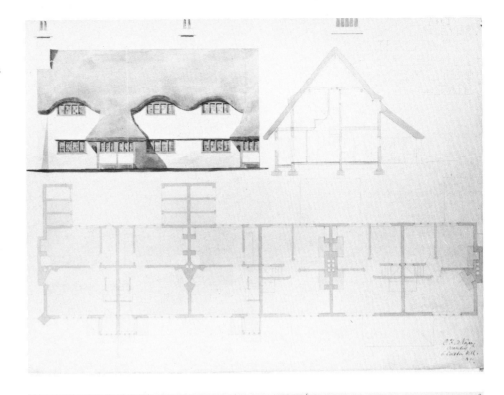

18
Design for a pair of thatched cottages at
Madresfield Court, Malvern Link, for the Earl
of Beauchamp, 1901. Elevations, sections and
plans. Unexecuted.

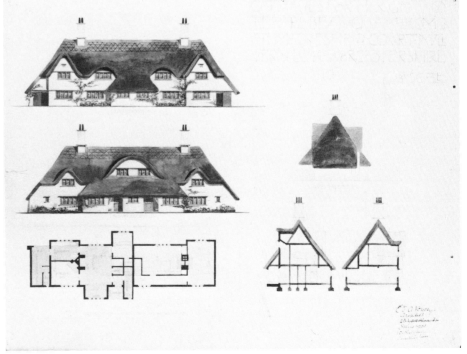

Design for a house and studio at Studland Bay,
Swanage, Dorset for A.Sutro, 1896. Front
elevation, substantially as executed; some
insensitive alterations to the house have now
been made.

now, their thatch replaced by slates applied after a fire in 1914, they seem very
ordinary. This does help to demonstrate a recurring feature of fascination for
Voysey; this was the way in which the arrangement of wall and roof in his houses
could be varied for visual effect. Its basis is an exaggeration of the possibilities of
the pitched roof form – the gable, the bay window and the dormer being placed in
eccentric relationship to the pitch of the roof. So in Voysey's work we see gutters
carried out and across in front of windows; roof pitches running down and around
projecting bays; or, as in the present instances, thatching being shaped around
fenestration in an unexpected and unorthodox way. This is something to bear in
mind as various houses are examined and as the rationale of Voysey's work is
discussed, for it is not an accidental, nor an unimportant feature. Indeed this
variety in the treatment of roofs, this emphasis on their importance, is one of the
dominant characteristics which emerge in the development of Edwardian
domestic architecture in the vernacular style.

If Greyfriars shows the way Voysey's work was moving in 1896 and
Elmesthorpe the scarcely hidden romanticism which overlay a desire to play with
conventional forms, then the studio for Sutro at Studland Bay was typical of the
small Voysey house of artistic pretensions. It shows a greater practice in coping
with the problems of site, a greater fluency, and is altogether an accomplished
building (19). It echoes the 'Small House for an Art Lover' which seems to have
been the staple for the first designs of Voysey's generation of Arts and Crafts
architects. Yet it also reminds us again that Voysey was by now several years into
his career as an architect and had acquired both clients and skills.

Norney

The 'proposed House for the Revd Leighton Grane at Shackleford, Surrey', appears in a first design dated May 1897 and was, as is noted on that drawing, 'discussed with Mr and Mrs Grane May 29th and 30th 1897'. The proposed house was to occupy a level site in open Surrey countryside, only two or three miles south of the recently built house on the Hog's Back. Ten miles south lies Haslemere where the other important house of this year, New Place, was to stand. It is apparent that on several occasions the building of one house in an area seems – as also at Malvern and on the shores of Lake Windermere – to have created a spate of work for Voysey. For a man whose clients often seemed to come to him in a haphazard way – one does not know at all, for instance, how the Revd Leighton Grane came to ask him to build a house – this does suggest quite strongly that people reacted locally to a house being built. They must have seen the house of a friend or acquaintance and as a result approached its architect and commissioned work for themselves. This, naturally, is the way in which much architectural commissioning will come; yet it seems too arbitrary a way in which to establish the practice of one of the best-known architects of a generation.

The first design for the Leighton Grane house, to be called Norney (20a), shows the house much as built. It has been suggested that Voysey's plans were fully worked out in his mind before he put pencil to paper and that he rarely altered a scheme. This is not generally so; there is ample evidence of the re-working of

20a
First design for Norney, near Shackleford, for the Revd W. Leighton Grane, 1897. With the exception of the polygonal bay and other details the plan shows the house as built; some elevational details differ.

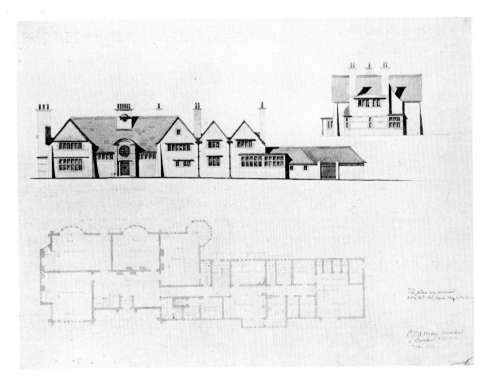

20b
The garden front of Norney.

schemes through several stages. The designs for the White Horse Inn at Stetchworth for the Earl of Ellesmere, designed in 1905, run through a whole series of re-drawings until Voysey finally emerges at a seventh revised plan. With Norney he does seem to have known what he wanted for there were only small changes of detail which differentiate this first proposal from the house as built (20b and 20c). In plan form the main house is unchanged although the finished house has a longer service wing, of three cross gables rather than two. Decorative and stylistic features have, however, been changed. Where the first drawing has three bow windows to the garden front the house has only two, with square gables over a round bow such as we will also see at Haslemere. The eccentric arrangement of the left-hand bow on the drawing, which wraps round the corner of the room in octagonal form, is lost. The prominent entrance porch is altered but remains in the same character. The south-east elevation (20d) has not, in the drawing, acquired the strong modelling which is one of the most interesting features of the house as built, with its ogee and semi-circular roof curves. These features turn what is

20c
Detail of the main entrance of Norney.

20d
The (south-east) end elevation of Norney.

basically a simple bay housing the ingle-nook into a dominant shaping of this end of the house. On the whole the house shows a strong symmetry and regularity on the garden front. There is a simplicity in this layout which is reflected in the, by now, standard use of roughcast and stone window dressings. Against this uniformity and sense of order are the several quite abrupt emphases: the heavy overhanging of the gables over the main window bays; the very prominent porch; and, echoing the shape of the porch on the end elevation, the bay already referred to. This sense of the dramatic in what is, after all, only a medium-size house is carried on inside in the very emphatic layout of the hall (20e). The ground plan and form of the house are otherwise, for Voysey, quite standard. The impression for the visitor is of a basic order overlaid with a strong eccentricity which gives the finished building a very pronounced and pleasant sense of tension. This certainly reflects the characteristic of the architect which we see also in his pattern designs, the interplay of a sense of order and a sense of fantasy and invention. At Norney we see another sign of it in the garden sundial (20f) of stone set on a column which

20e
Contemporary photograph of the hall at
Norney, showing the double-storey height
and avoidance of diagonals.

20f
Detail of the garden sundial at Norney; it is of
stone on an octagonal base, the support cross-
shaped in section with an identical grotesque
profile carved into each arm of the cross.
Believed to be contemporary with the house.

is a four-sided profile grotesque caricature, possibly based (Voysey's caricatures
often though not always were) on his client's face. This use of the grotesque has
already been seen in the porch of the studio for Britten (see 7b) with its wooden
supports shaped to a caricature head and will be seen in several future designs, both
of furniture and of fixtures for houses.

In plan Norney shows a cluster of rooms grouped around the hall with the
service rooms added in a long line continuing along the garden front. The hall
itself is a large area, two floors in height with a gallery landing. This hall best
exemplifies Voysey's ideas on the hall in domestic houses, which he expressed in an
article in the *Studio*; he writes:

> Spaciousness and ample superficial area are essential qualities in a good
> hall, the effect of which excessive height tends to limit and destroy. The
> horizontal lines of a gallery or of long, low beams will contribute
> towards the effect of spaciousness and repose. For the same reason all
> diagonal lines should be avoided, such as ramping or raking handrails
> and strings, all of which tend to destroy repose. Whatever size the hall
> may be, its length and width should have preeminence over its height.[1]

This is very much the line and style of argument that Voysey was to develop in all
his polemics; the key words we grow to recognise are repeated and hammered
home as 'repose' is here. Even while we recognise the force and sincerity of the
argument we are aware of a certain eccentricity, especially when we come upon
such statements as:

> It is the modern craze for high rooms (originating in foreign travel)
> which has led to the destruction of all effects of repose. Doors,
> windows and even furniture appear as if 'stood on end'. Verticality and
> unrest are our gods![2]

Voysey never travelled abroad; it is doubtful whether his journeys outside Britain exceeded a long weekend in Holland with members of the Art Workers' Guild. In addition to the idiosyncrasy of this remark Voysey also introduces here one of his major and recurring themes, the relationship between 'verticality' and the effect of 'unrest'. This idea runs through his work and will emerge again and again. Another emphatic remark in this article on the domestic hall, relevant to Norney as to all Voysey houses, is:

> The effect of spaciousness and repose cannot be produced by the
> contents of old curiosity shops. You must choose your hall furniture
> and ornaments as carefully as you choose the first words to a stranger
> on his arrival, if you would produce on him an effect of peaceful
> friendship and homely bliss.[3]

These are the beginnings of the developed Voysey argument that the home is chiefly a place of comfort, not of show, for the inhabitant and a place of welcome for the visitor or guest.

New Place

Towards the end of 1897 Voysey was at work on the proposed house at Haslemere, a few miles south of Norney; his client was A.M.M.Stedman, who had founded in 1889 the publishing firm of Methuen and Co. In 1899 Stedman assumed the surname Methuen which accounts for some confusion over the client's name. In 1916 he became Sir Algernon Methuen, and lived at New Place until his death in 1924. His house was designed in 1897 with various outbuildings – cottage, summer house, motor-house – added in the next few years; it has a formal garden layout designed by Voysey, partly with the house, partly in 1901. New Place has the advantage over Norney of a sloping site; the house is orientated east-west with the main entrance on the west side and the main rooms facing south. Since the site falls away quite steeply to the west this provides the opportunity, which Voysey always seemed to enjoy and to respond to, for differing levels and terracing. Thus, for instance, the south or terrace front has a doorway leading from the hall to a terrace into which two short wings – housing the drawing-room and study – project (21a,b). The study has a single-storey bay front with curved, leaded roof. The drawing-room has a bay, also round, which like the garden front bays at Norney rises up two storeys to a projecting gable. Here, though, the bay also drops below the terrace to a third level; so although the flanking wings to the hall are in plan balanced, they vary in elevation from one to three storeys in height. New Place also, like Norney but unlike most of the later houses, favours consistent use of the curve. There is a round-headed porch to the front door, echoed in a semi-circular drip course on the adjacent chimney-stack (21c), which exactly reflects the form used over the ingle-nook at Norney. Against this curve is contrasted a square, flat-roofed ground-floor bay and the row of three bedroom

21a
New Place (originally called Hurtmore) at
Haslemere for A.M.M.Stedman, later Sir
Algernon Methuen, 1897. The terrace front,
showing the terrace wall, the three-storey bay
window and, to the left, the entrance front.

21b
The terrace front of New Place, from the
terrace.

21c
The entrance front and main door of New
Place; the arched porch rests on stone corbels
carved into each of which can be seen a
grotesque profile. The typical down-pipe
brackets and castellated hopper also show
clearly, as used on many of Voysey's houses.

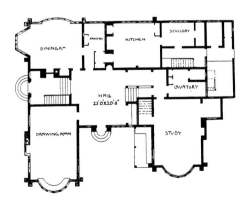

21d
The ground-floor plan of New Place.

53

Contemporary drawing of the hall at New
Place showing the three arched openings,
balanced by the chimney-piece to the left.

windows which break the line of the projecting eaves as they break up into the
roof slope, each with its small flat roof. On the terrace front (21b) is a similar
contrast; the curved roof to the bay already mentioned and the adjacent curved
garden arch are set against a row of three gables at different heights, that over the
door having a projecting bell housing echoing the large projecting gable adjacent.
There is a further curve to the drip course on the chimney-stack rising above this
door. New Place is approached by a curved drive and this, and the slope of the site,
hides the house until the visitor is quite near. It also has the roughcast finish and
stone dressings which we can now take for granted as features of the developing
Voysey house.

The plan form (21d) and internal arrangements of New Place reflect that it is the
most elaborate house Voysey ever built, with lavish internal fitments though
unfortunately he was not given a free hand to use his own moveable furniture.
Despite this considerable scale of attention and expenditure in internal fittings the
layout and idiom are very close to Norney. Stylistically, the hall (21e) shows the
half-round motif taken from the exterior and repeated, in the chimney-piece, the
fender and the row of three round-headed arches. One leads through to the study,
the centre one leads direct to the stairs, the third is blind with panelling and a bench
seat. The same repeat of the half-round motif from outside has been seen in the hall
at Norney, though otherwise the two halls are very different in character. At New
Place, again as at Norney, the main rooms are grouped around the entrance hall,
the drawing-room and study forming two flanking projecting wings on the
terrace front to which reference has already been made. The hall is of conventional
ceiling height which is to say, it has the relatively low ceiling that Voysey always

favoured – except where he deliberately used a double-storey height – even in the largest of his rooms. The large and prominent chimney-piece demonstrates effectively that Voysey thought of the hall as an area to be used, not simply a place of reception and circulation; it was the focal point of the house. He has emphasized this at New Place by having the main entrance, the garden entrance, the stairs and main rooms all opening directly off it. There was at the turn of the century a considerable sense among the more progressive of the domestic architects of the importance of the hall, expressed not in practical but more in emotional terms. This was founded clearly on a sense of the past, on a conception of the domestic building in particular of Tudor England – but not primarily the Tudor of romantically whimsical half-timbering, though this played some part. Voysey offered as his contribution the article quoted above, in which he also said:

> The hall should receive its guests with composure and dignity, but still
> with brightness, open arms and warmth; warmth of colour as rich and
> luxurious as you like but above all things sober and resposeful . . .[4]

M.H.Baillie Scott also contributed at some length to this debate; his sense of the English tradition of the hall was based more firmly on an historical sense than Voysey's, which rested on the demonstrable need for the kind of facilities which his halls offered. Baillie Scott writes:

> Of late years there has been a great revival of the hall as a central feature
> in a house . . . the hall is to be a place where the family may assemble
> round the fire in the evening, without being disturbed by servants
> passing through it, or without being obliged to hastily decamp on the
> arrival of an unwelcome visitor.[5]

This was written in 1895; a few years later Baillie Scott again took this subject up in the *Studio*:

> In seeking for a basis for the plan of a small house it may be well to
> follow the evolution of the complex modern house; and in tracing this
> back to its source it will be found that it originally comprised but one
> apartment – the hall or house-place, as it was called – and if its
> development from this primary form is followed it will be found that it
> consisted chiefly in the formation of special cells for special purposes.[6]

He comments that from the original hall-house the prominence and physical size of the hall dwindled with its importance. Eventually it became a mere 'lobby' until in 'modern times':

> . . . amidst other features and details of the past, the hall became again a
> somewhat notable feature in the plan and was considered almost an
> essential adjunct to the 'artistic house'.[7]

A similar argument, in more detail, is put by Charles Harrison Townsend in his Introduction to a book which was reprinted by the *Studio* in 1901, indicating the public and professional demand for information on the topic. This was Nash's *The Mansions of England in the Olden Time*.[8] Harrison Townsend, in his own highly successful architectural practice, played as big a part as Voysey and Baillie Scott in establishing the hall as a strong feature of much domestic architecture of these years.

Both Norney and New Place were substantial and successful works which finally established Voysey as a recognized domestic architect; they also demonstrated that he was, as in the way outlined above, contributing to the practice of domestic architecture in accordance with the progressive architectural thought of his age. His houses of 1896–7, of which the two discussed above are the most important, show a definite sense of tradition and also a willingness to innovate. The blend which has been referred to, of simplicity with a richness of feature which was muted in most of Voysey's later work, was a part of his development, separating him from the relative eclecticism of his first years of practice and the further maturing of his style in the last two years of the century. With the building of Norney and New Place in 1897, Voysey made a place for himself in the history of British architecture.

Experiments in furniture, 1895–7

In April 1894, as we have seen, Voysey was telling the members of the RIBA that he was 'groping in the dark, struggling to find out the true laws which govern fitness and beauty'[9] for the design of furniture. This was the cry from the heart of a young designer; in the same talk he came a little closer to the practicalities of the problem when he said:

> We must restrain the carver, the inlayer, the polisher and the metal-
> worker and be careful that the thought in their design is as good as its
> execution. Also encourage them to concentrate ornament, and cease to
> use it as a means of hiding cheap construction and bad workmanship
> and material.[10]

To put this remark in perspective, it was made in a climate where the progressive movement in furniture design was already much as Voysey suggested it might be. The Art Workers' Guild, of which he had been a member for a decade, was setting the right standards; C.R.Ashbee and the Guild of Handicraft were at work and in the public eye; the Arts and Crafts Exhibition Society had also been founded for a decade and its influential and well-publicised exhibitions were promulgating standards of taste which on the whole conformed to Voysey's wishes. The list of designers and craftsmen who were established in this kind of work goes back as far as the Aesthetic Movement starting in the 1870s and including E.W.Godwin and Christopher Dresser; Voysey's own mentor Arthur Heygate Mackmurdo had been producing ten years previously clean uncluttered oak furniture, largely devoid of ornament and relying on cleanness of line for its effect. In Voysey's own generation there were designers like himself set to produce good furniture, men like Walter Cave and M.H.Ballie Scott. There were also the firms of artist-craftsmen like A.W.Simpson of Kendal, set up in 1889, who would do a great deal of work with and for Voysey. It was a busy field in which Voysey chose to participate and he entered it with an enthusiasm and a disregard for opposition or competition typical of all his work. One of the outstanding features of Voysey's furniture designs is the use of bronze or brass fittings – a range of hinges, door handles and knobs, locks, escutcheons, keys – to his own design; these were made by the firm of Elsley and Co. and it is a mark of the success of these designs that they became a commercially available range of items. Voysey had realized the

Design for a clock case in softwood, 1895, the decoration to be applied in oil colour. Various colour and other notes can just be made out, and a price of £1.10s for the woodwork from Cootes.

Contemporary photograph of a wooden barometer and thermometer, c.1895, case hand-painted in oil colour.

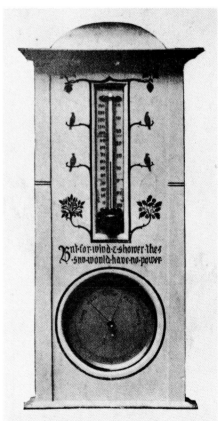

BAROMETER AND   C. F. A. VOYSEY
THERMOMETER CASE

24
The bedroom of The Orchard at
Chorleywood, c.1900, from a contemporary
photograph. The bed, chest of drawers and
bedside cupboard are by Voysey; also the
carpet, candlesticks and fire-irons; and the
cast-iron chimney-piece which is identical to
that shown in detail in 30g.

importance of such details as this in the early 1890s; in the drawings for Perrycroft,
for instance, is a design for the elaborate front-door hinges for that house. There is
also a design made for that house of two of the most often repeated fittings: a strap
hinge terminating in a heart shape incised with the outline of a bird eating a
cherry, and the small, slender profiled knob which became a standard fitting for all
cupboard doors and drawers. This drawing, though undated, is in a run of
Perrycroft drawings dated from Dec. 1893–Jan. 1894.

In the design of houses the years 1895–7 were experimental in that Voysey,
searching for accomplishment in his work, adopted a style of work which he later
dropped. In his designs for furniture and interior fittings those same years were
experimental in that he evolved, from the few and slightly inelegant furniture
designs of earlier years which we have seen above, the basis of the complete range
of furniture which he was to produce for the rest of his life. By 1898 most of the
recognizable and distinctive Voysey furniture designs had appeared; the years
1895–7 laid a very solid foundation for these.

1895 began with a design which is not typical, but is one of the most distinctive
and best known of Voysey's output. It is a clock-case originally made for himself,
though possibly repeated in this form for a friend; a case of similar form was also
produced in small quantities without the decoration and in aluminium. Softwood,
rare for Voysey, was used for the original and the distinctive feature is the
elaborate hand-painting, by Voysey himself (22). The design is dated Jan. 1895 and
there is a sister design (23), similar in form though attenuated and less elaborately

25
Contemporary line drawing of a writing desk,
designed 1895 for W. Ward Higgs; the metal
fittings are of brass, the incised panel originally
laid, the design for the piece notes, on 'blood
red leather'.

26
Hanging cupboard and bookshelves, pre-1896,
to a design made for the Home Arts and
Industries Association. Various features are
unusual, not least the pressed metal strap
hinges and fittings, which differ in detail from
those shown on the design and from any other
of Voysey's metalwork.

27
Contemporary photograph of a bedroom
chair, designed 1896, the frame to be either
softwood or oak, the seat of canvas slung like a
deck-chair. Note the grotesque profile
cutaways in the sides. The client is not known
and the piece is not known to survive. It was
made by A. W. Simpson.

painted, for a barometer case. Both designs are architectural in their form, which
favours plain surface, clearly expressed construction and simple moulding.

Also from 1895 are designs for a bed and chest of drawers which are shown (24)
in Voysey's own bedroom at The Orchard, his house at Chorleywood (see 35).
The bed is a good example of a repeated design; in 1895 one was made for
Horniman, presumably for use at Lowicks; a second and third were made over the
next half-dozen years, one for Moor Crag at Windermere (see 30) and the third, as
shown, for Voysey himself. The three are identical, the design for each being
traced afresh with the name of the new client added. These designs for bed and
chest of drawers were typical and instantly recognizable as Voysey's work though
distinctively part of his early output. The bed with its tall capped posts belongs
clearly, too clearly for Voysey's mature taste, to the Mackmurdo tradition; the
chest of drawers, sturdy and solid, is reminiscent of such early work by Voysey as
the massive table of 1889 shown above (11).

If the small hand-painted clock-case (above) is the best-known small Voysey
piece then another design of the same year – the design is dated Feb. 1895 – is surely
the best known, though again not the most typical, large piece. This is the oak
bureau or 'Writing Table' (as it is described on the design) made for W. Ward
Higgs. For Ward Higgs Voysey carried out, at 23 Queensborough Terrace in
London, the fully fitted interior from which much of the best surviving Voysey
furniture comes. The bureau (25) stands on slender legs of octagonal section – the
device of chamfering the supports from square to octagonal section, used here and
on the bed described above, became a distinctive trademark – which continue to

the height of the moulded cornice at the top of the bureau. The carcase is slung between them, supported at desk-top and cornice level. The elegant lines of the piece are enhanced by a decorative panel in incised brass originally laid, the design notes, on blood-red leather. The panel depicts one of Voysey's beloved pastoral scenes of a strong medieval flavour. It is stressed on the design that the brasswork is not to be lacquered. Voysey does not, in this instance, specify the finish of the timber but we can take it that it was to be left clean, 'without stain or polish'. In conjunction with the unlacquered brass which would quickly dull we get a clear picture of a piece finished in scrubbed, clean oak and dull, greyish brasswork. This is how a piece of Voysey furniture was, without doubt, intended by its designer to look.

Another piece of furniture appeared in 1896 which, though distinctive and appealing like the bed and drawers, represented an unsuccessful experiment. This was the hanging cupboard and bookshelves (26). Its fascination may be that it reveals the beginnings of Voysey's working and social relationship with A.W.Simpson, the furniture designer and maker of Kendal. Certainly they had met by 1896; the A.W.Simpson firm had been established in 1886, and there is a strong resemblance between this piece and several to Simpson's own design included in his trade catalogues. It seems likely that in designing this piece Voysey was influenced by Simpson's work and tried something new. Neither before nor after did he produce anything similar; the carved medievalized figures surmounting the piece do recur in his work, as does the low-relief carving, but the form of the piece does not. It was made up, in 1896 at the latest though possibly earlier, for the Home Arts and Industries Association; it was in oak and it is noted on the design: 'These figures [i.e. the two figures surmounting the piece] to be very squarely cut and not at all realistic in detail'.

Bearing in mind that these were years of experiment and of forming a style the final piece of furniture in this chapter (27) may not come as a surprise. In form it resembles a porter's chair though, as an appreciative writer in the *Artist* notes, that was not the intended use:

> The painted bedroom chair looks cumbersome, but is not. Being very
> light in make and on castors it moves with a touch. This chair would be
> invaluable to an invalid, it is so snugly protected from draughts, and
> the slung seat is most comfortable, yielding as it does to every
> movement of the body.[11]

It stands on four corner supports, full height and round in section, infilled on three sides with planked panels and capped with an overhanging canopy. The infill panels are relieved by curved bottom edges and cutaways at the side outlining a grotesque head. The seat is slung canvas, the woodwork probably deal, painted a pale blue-green (the drawing for this piece, dated Feb. 1896, includes quotations for construction in both oak and deal; the chair is illustrated in the *Studio*[12] as by Simpson, whose quotation is for deal construction). Whatever the intention of this idiosyncratic piece – the drawing describes it as a 'bedroom chair', the inference presumably being that in the chilly bedroom of one's Voyseyesque 'House for an

Art Lover' one needed to be shielded from draughts – it is fascinating. Whether more than one was made is not known; certainly it is not known to survive and the drawing – contrary to Voysey's usual practice – does not name a client. The assumption therefore is that it was made speculatively by Simpson for the 1896 Arts and Crafts Exhibition at which it was shown.

To conclude this chapter here are some comments from the columns of Voysey's enthusiastic and consistent champion, the *Studio*:

> For if few people can afford to have furniture specially designed for
> them, there are still fewer who, having the means, possess also the taste
> to put the idea into execution and courage enough to face the result. To
> have a room furnished differently from those of one's neighbours
> would seem to be considered an affectation today – or at least, the
> worst crime known to 'society' – bad form. Otherwise we might find
> Mr Voysey's services had been secured, not by a few here and there,
> but by many an owner of the palaces constantly springing up in
> London.[13]

We have no great knowledge of Voysey's views on 'society'; he is said to have been inclined to snobbery, very aware of the social standing of his client. He never seems to have pressed for duplication of his designs though we know that one of his most favoured furniture makers, F.C.Nielsen, did go into limited commercial production with one or two designs. So, flattering as the above comments were, they might not have found favour with the designer, particularly with their implication that it might in any sense be considered bad form to have a roomful of Voysey's furniture! More perceptively the same writer comments:

> If you can appreciate the reticence and severity of Mr Voysey's work,
> you can no longer tolerate the ordinary commercially designed
> product. His furniture deserves elaborate and patient study, for its one
> aim is 'proportion, proportion, proportion' and that is a quality most
> elusive and difficult even to appreciate, much less to achieve.[14]

Voysey's own words, reflecting his view at this point in his career, included the comment:

> Simplicity in decoration is one of the most essential qualities without
> which no true richness is possible. To know where to stop and what
> not to do is a long way on the road to being a great decorator.[15]

The sort of issues raised here – the value of simplicity, the use of ornament, uniqueness versus quantity production, standards of commercial design – all come together in another of those unusual projects with which Voysey was sometimes associated. Again this appeared at the 1896 Arts and Crafts Exhibition and again we have no idea how it was originated; a model was exhibited and there is no reason to believe that it ever went into production:

> A striking instance of a commonplace item of daily life made artistic by
> virtue of fine properties is the lamp-post shown in a model, by Mr
> Voysey. Unless you regard the emblazoned arms of the City of London
> as decoration, it owes little to ornament. But the square lantern, and the
> harmonious balance of the various component parts, must not be
> overlooked. A hundred men could ornament a lamp-post, but very

few could design one. This instance of an artist's power to embody a
fresh idea without departing unduly from an accepted type, supplies as
good a moral as the show affords.[16]

Whether the object is a house, a writing desk or a lamp-post Voysey is now taking
a very firm stand in his design work; his ideals are proportion and simplicity allied
to quality of workmanship; without any perversity or sense of irony he can see
simplicity as an essential quality of richness. He carries us along with these views,
which defines in fact why his work still appears so striking and successful. He
certainly seems to have swayed his contemporaries for by 1896 one of them can
write:

> The 1896 Exhibition does justice to this artist, and he fully supports our
> expectations; for, despite treading now and then on firmly established
> prejudices, his vivid personality is one of the chief factors in modern
> design – one that cannot fail to have immense influence on the design of
> the coming century.[18]

The value of contemporary critical comment can be ambiguous; it is a
commonplace that often the age in which work is carried out or innovations made
cannot accurately judge its worth; a commonplace also that critics do not really
know their stuff. This does not seem true of the year under discussion where,
allowing for the occasional flight of extravagant fancy, the critics seem to have
their standards clearly established and their judgements sound. The *Studio*, for
instance, inclines to praise rather than to blame and we must bear that in mind.
However it also inclines to praise Voysey more consistently and highly than most
of his contemporaries. The judgement that it, and other periodicals, offer us on the
progress of Voysey's career is sound and valuable. Just as important is the insight
that they offer, often by allusive comment rather than direct statement, as to what
was, in those years, seen as the norm and what was an original departure from that
norm. It is reassuring that the things we find to be fresh and startling about
Voysey's work – or so we think – were thought equally original when first
designed. The comments of contemporary critics therefore offer a valuable
yardstick, the comparison of their own judgements with ours providing a truer
evaluation both of what was going on and of its significance.

Chapter 4 The Years of Mature Practice, 1898–1910

After 1897 Voysey's practice entered its busiest period; even so, in terms of the career of a very well-known architect, the years of hectic business were relatively few. It is apparent that by 1904 the rush was easing off rapidly and the houses built between then and 1910, though including some important work, do not contain anything to the standard of Broadleys (1898), Moor Crag (1898), Spade House (1899), the Sandersons factory (1902), Vodin (1903) or the Whitwood Institute (1904). Then as the first decade of the century passed there was a distinct change as, in the houses of 1909 such as at Combe Down or Henley-in-Arden, a distinct element of Gothic detailing crept in, indicating what was to become a strong element in Voysey's later work. It is tempting to suggest a parallel with the architect whose principles and integrity Voysey appeared to admire most, A.W.N.Pugin; for though Pugin, the great Catholic Revival architect, died young at 40 in 1852 whereas Voysey lived to be 83, Pugin's major work was almost entirely done in the decade from 1840 to 1850, Voysey's from 1895 to 1905. Both lived in those ten years a life of hectic effort which, in both cases, adversely affected their general health. The drama and sheer pace of Pugin's brief career exceeds that of his later fellow but the comparisons are more than passing.

1898 began with a proposal for a client named Newbold for a house in Sussex, just north of Brighton in the small village of Westmeston. The house was not built, the failure being symbolic for it was in the mould of Norney and New Place which Voysey had now outlived: big, lavish, with a corner tower, three polygonal bays and an elaborated porch (28). Unusually, the roof was to have been of red tiles though otherwise, in roughcast with stone dressings, the finish was as expected. The design for this is dated March; by the middle of that year two of the best-known houses were on the drawing board. Both were sited, within a few hundred yards of each other, in one of the most picturesque areas in the country, on the edge of Lake Windermere in the Lake District. Because they are very different houses and because, as the drawings show, the designs were evolved within a few days of each other, the decision as to which to discuss first is arbitrary.

Broadleys

The house called Broadleys is spectacularly situated on a levelled site on the very edge of the lake; in front of the terrace on which the house stands the ground falls sharply away to the water's edge with a clear view across to the west side of the

28
Design for a house at Westmeston, Sussex, for
A.Newbold, 1898; perspective drawings with
watercolour of front and rear plus plans.
Unexecuted.

64

Broadleys on Lake Windermere for A.Currer Briggs, 1898. This shows the house seen from the lake itself with the three bow windows and the service wing to the left.

lake. This situation has produced the most often published single elevation of all Voysey's work, the lake-front of the house with its three two-storey, deep, semi-circular bow windows (29a), which ironically can only be properly seen from the middle of the lake. As built the house is a simple L-shape, the ends terminated with hipped roofs; the hipped roof is repeated in the staircase extension of two storeys which sits in the angle of the L, behind the main lake-front elevation. Next to this, hard up against the angle (29b) is a gabled extension housing the porch and entrance lobby. The contrast of this gable, echoed in the small porch, with the hipped roof and horizontal band of windows tucked up under the eaves gives an interest to the entrance front which belies the very simple arrangement of the house. The longer arm of the L, slightly lower than the other and running back from the lake, is a service wing. The main wing houses at ground-floor level three rooms, in a row and interlinking, the dining-room, drawing-room and hall which, originally, housed a billiard table(29c). In the first scheme (29d), drawn up in June 1898, the buildings occupied three sides of a square, the fourth being closed by a hedge; this would have been a more substantial house with, for instance, a separate billiard-room. So the final scheme, drawn out in July, simplifies and reduces the layout. The house as seen today follows this July layout and remains externally as built except that the south end of the main wing has been filled in where originally a bedroom overhung the verandah.

Broadleys was built for a client called Currer Briggs; he was the son of the Henry Briggs who owned the colliery at Whitwood, near Normanton in Yorkshire where Voysey later carried out work. The company was clearly a

29b
Broadleys, the entrance porch and staircase
extension. To the left, partly obscured by
bushes, can be seen the infill where the
verandah used to be.

BROADLEYS : WINDERMERE
FOR A CVRRER BRIGGS ESQ

29c
Contemporary perspective watercolour, with inset plans, of Broadleys as executed.

progressive one for it employed Voysey to build housing and an Institute for its employees, begun in 1905. There is a certain oddity in this for whatever else he may have been Voysey was no progressive in his social views. In his mind no doubt there were feudal overtones to the scheme. However, at Broadleys Mr Currer Briggs was in his summer house and at leisure and the house reflects this. As we grow to expect of Voysey, and as indicated above, there are surprises in the comparison of the two main elevations, lake and entrance. The entrance front sets several elements side by side; as the visitor enters from the road he first sees the bedroom window projecting up into the hip, the gutter bracketted across in front of it; then, moving round, the contrasts of the entrance area as described above. Coming then to the lakeside, he sees the completely different mood of the large, dominant bows and their detailing (29e). Again, as we have seen in other buildings and will see again, Voysey creates variety by playing with levels. The bows push up through the wide projecting eaves into the roof pitch, which weaves around the capping cornice and spreads around the curve. The little round window with its curved drip course, set in emphatic stone dressings, picks up the strong motif of

67

29d
Design for the first scheme for Broadleys,
dated June 1898; south elevation (the lake
would lie to the west) with ground plan.

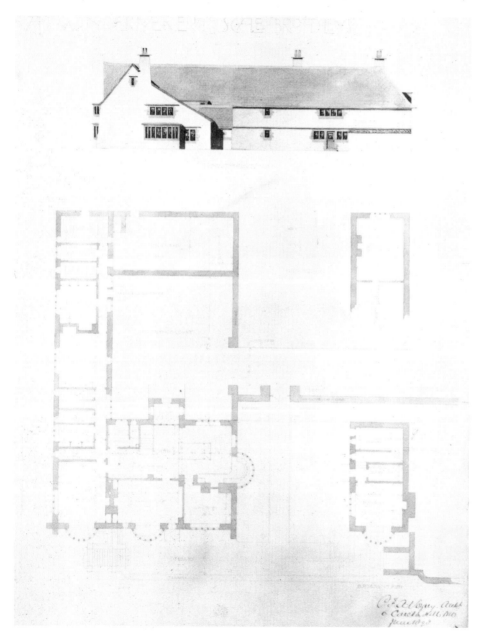

29e (right)
Detail of the lakeside (west) front of Broadleys.

29f (left)
Detail of the oak staircase of Broadleys, from the half-landing between ground and first floors.

29g (left, below)
Detail of the carved oak grotesque corbel from the hall at Broadleys; this is presumed to be a caricature of Currer Briggs, Voysey's client. The figure is less than life-size and carved in the coarse style that Voysey favoured for such work, the tool marks remaining in the wood.

29h
Contemporary photograph showing the dining-room at Broadleys shortly after the house was completed, with furniture largely to Voysey's own designs in situ.

29i
The Lodge at Broadleys, a detail showing the stone construction without mortar and wooden casements.

curves which dominates this aspect of the house. The whole effect is, in its spectacular setting, unique in Voysey's work and very effective.

Moving inside the house the sense of solidity, comfort and successful design, offset by the odd surprise, continues. A lobby leads through into the hall, off which runs a staircase (29f). Here, as he recommends for entrance halls, Voysey has avoided any use of diagonals. The rails are inset with a green inlay, a unique decoration in Voysey's work; joinery here is all oak. The hall itself rises through the height of two storeys. It is panelled and gives a splendid view over the lake.

The only surprise comes on looking back from the window to the gallery containing the first-floor passage to the bedrooms; for on each heavy oak corbel is a carved grotesque (29g), the carving deliberately coarse, stylized and evocative, one assumes, of the appearance and character of Mr Currer Briggs himself. There was originally a good deal of Voysey's own designed furniture in the house; Hermann Muthesius, the German government representative who produced in the first decade of the present century a comprehensive and interesting account of the state of English contemporary domestic architecture,[1] devoted some space to Broadleys, a house which he admired. Indeed he admired Voysey's work in general. He includes among others a photograph of the dining-room in its original state which shows the furniture in situ (29h).

In addition to the main building Broadleys has an entrance lodge, also by Voysey (29i), which is built in the local vernacular tradition; in fact this blends extraordinarily well with Voysey's style of design and produces an extremely effective little building which avoids the temptation to which Voysey sometimes succumbed of producing contrived and whimsical effects.

Broadleys is an extremely effective and distinctive house in which the architect has responded enthusiastically to the excellent opportunity afforded by the location. He has produced a house of simple layout, just sufficiently offset by emphatic and varied detailing; internally it is of great comfort and quality, again offset by details which give it distinction and a sense of lightness. If we leave Broadleys and move just a few hundred yards south along the lakeside road we come to the drive into another house which deals with the problem of site in a completely different and, in some ways, more thoughtful and successful manner. Broadleys is a very well-contrived house put down on a levelled terrace overlooking the lake. Moor Crag is a house built into its site, set further back, higher up and on a slope.

Moor Crag

The house is not visible from the road; it is approached by a curving drive which runs through grounds landscaped at the time of the house's building by Mawson. The first design for the house (30a) shows that it was worked up on lines very similar to Broadleys; this is hardly surprising since this initial design, dated July 1898, must have been in Voysey's mind concurrently with Broadleys itself. So the first plan is for an L-shaped layout, a square bay and two angled bays on the garden front and a porch and a staircase extension built into the angle of the L. Internally the differences are more pronounced, particularly since a transverse division creates a passage at ground-floor level off which the main rooms lead. This suggests that Voysey did not wish to repeat the galleried, two-storey-high hall of Broadleys. This is confirmed by the second design (30b) which shows a basically similar layout for the ground-floor main rooms, though the porch now gives directly onto the hall, which has been reduced in width to alter the proportions of the front and so needs the extension in depth. The considerable change in this second plan is that the service wing has been turned through ninety degrees to produce a rectangular layout. Seen in elevation this permits some moves towards

30a
Ground-floor plan for the first scheme for a
house for J.W.Buckley at Windermere, dated
1898.

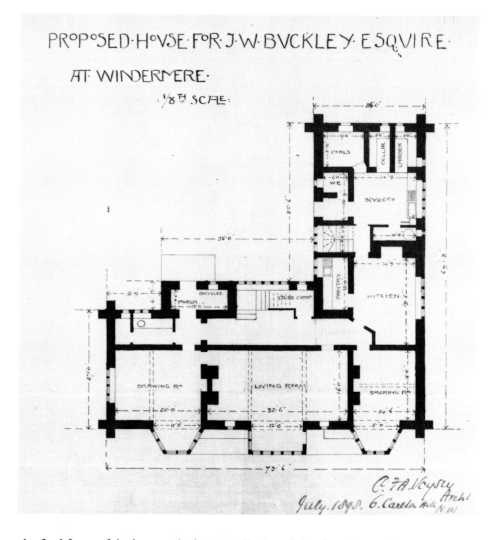

the final form of the house; the basic similarity of the elevation to the main rooms
with that at Broadleys persists, with the two flanking bays breaking through the
roofline and the pitch of the roof sweeping down below eaves level between them.
The middle, square bay is now recessed at first-floor level so lies between being a
bay and a dormer. The orientation of this drawing is not clear (and, indeed, there
are one or two inconsistencies in the relationship between plan and elevation) but
we can assume that it would more or less be that of the house as built, which is east-
west at right angles to the lake. This means that the sweep down of the gable over
the front door is echoing the slope of the surrounding land to that end of the house.
This emphasizes the second, and most important, change in the conception of the
house which is apparent in the third and final design (30c); this design, for the first
time, acknowledges the slope of the site, which is shown to fall away at the service
end of the house (the west). This is emphasized (30d) by the long sweep of the roof

30b
Design showing the second scheme for a house
for J.W.Buckley at Windermere, 1898; front
and rear elevations and plans.

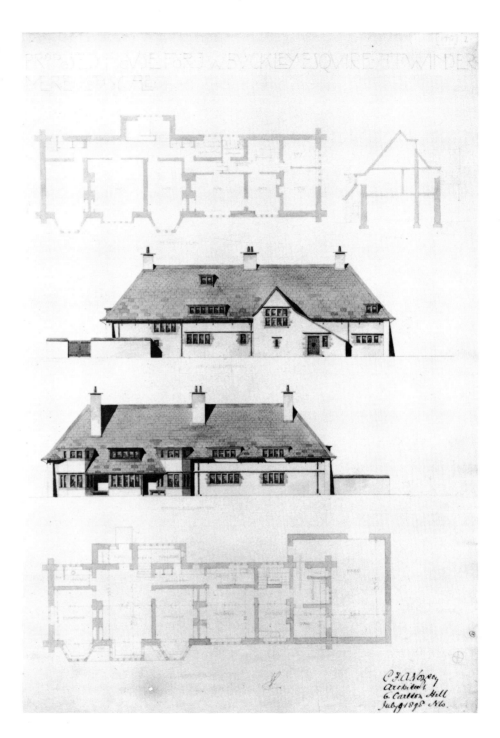

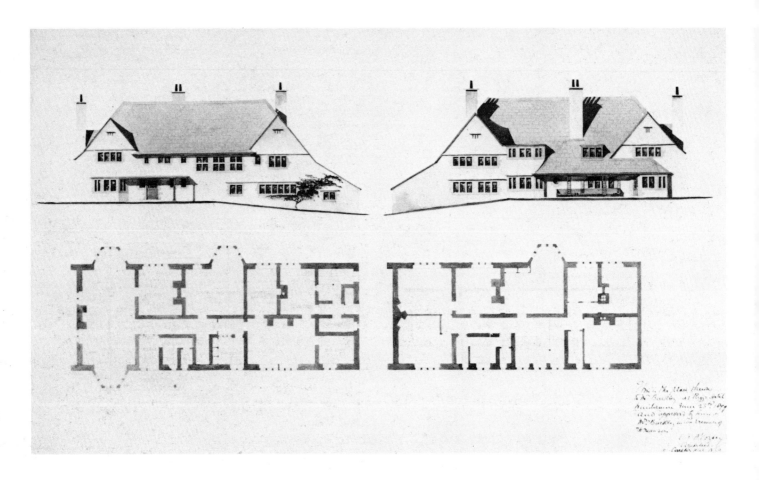

30c
Design as executed for Moor Crag at
Windermere for J.W.Buckley, 1899; front and
rear elevations and plans. It is noted in
Voysey's hand on the drawing that this scheme
was approved by the client in the presence of
Mawson, who laid out the grounds, in June
1899. The name Moor Crag does not appear
on the design.

right down to head height at this end of the building and further emphasized in the
elevation by the fact that this end is gabled, standing out clearly against the slate
roof which runs down to first-floor level over the verandah along the rest of this
garden front. The regularity of the garden front, already broken, is further
disrupted by the insertion of the two-storey bay, flat roofed and now, though not
originally, with a tile-hung apron. On the entrance front one is also very aware of
the downhill sweep of both house and site, and this is the impression one gets
approaching up the drive. But seen from the front Voysey has chosen to
emphasize the symmetry of the house which, on the other elevation, he had
equally chosen to break.

In plan also this house has moved far away from the first two, Broadleys-based,
designs. At the east end the long dining-room runs transversely the full width of
the house, perhaps recognizing a need for at least one room which looked out in
both directions, both at the natural setting and at the carefully landscaped gardens
in the Picturesque tradition. Otherwise the emphasis is taken off the entrance front
which consists of service rooms and staircase, a corridor set more or less centrally
and running the length of the house providing access to rooms. The staircase,

30d
Moor Crag, the garden front.

30e
Moor Crag, the staircase from the first-floor landing.

30f
Moor Crag, the chimney-piece in the drawing-room; the woodwork is all oak, the fender brass and the small tiles have a gold lustre glaze. The cast-iron ventilator grille above, with an incised design of birds and trees, is a recurring feature throughout this and many other houses.

30g
Moor Crag, a cast-iron bedroom chimney-piece typical of those which appear in many of Voysey's houses.

30h
The coach house and stables located opposite the drive entrance leading up to Moor Crag.

though less elaborate than that at Broadleys, is very much in Voysey's best and plainest style (30e). Great use is made throughout of oak panelling and the house contains some fine chimney-pieces (30f) and excellent examples of the plain, cast-iron bedroom fireplaces (30g). Opposite the entrance to the drive is a coach-house (30h).

It is highly instructive of Voysey's working style to watch the evolution of this house; the final design is dated with the comment, in Voysey's hand, 'This is the plan shown to Mr Buckley at Rigg's Hotel, Windermere, June 23rd 1899 and approved by him and Mrs Buckley in the presence of Mr Mawson'. Mr Buckley, the client, was clearly a man who knew what he wanted and was prepared to negotiate for almost a year to get it. It is interesting also to see that Thomas H.Mawson, the landscape gardener, was very much part of the process at this stage and that gardener and architect were working in close touch. It was undoubtedly the care and thought that went into Moor Crag, transmuting it from the earlier scheme to the final one, that made it the achievement it was. Although we know nothing of Buckley and the relationship he set up with Voysey, the development of this, the most successful and typical Voysey house, dispels the common assumption that Voysey was an inflexible man who sat at his drawing board, mapped out a finished design in a sitting of a few hours and then built it. There are several other, important instances where we see his development of a design through several stages but Moor Crag is the best and most effective. It has now an enormous air of appropriateness in its setting; it is a comfortable house and an attractive one; it has a basic discipline of layout treated with enough variety to create strong interest; it was also sufficiently financed to make all the fittings, though plain, of high quality. In its relationship to its setting, its detail of design, its quality of finish and its character it is the single most successful house that Voysey designed and built.

A third house was in the process of being drawn out at the same time as the two Windermere houses; this was a proposal for a house in Collington Avenue, Bexhill, Sussex, for a client named A.Barker and the first design is dated June 1898. A slightly modified second scheme (31) shows a house with certain similarities to Broadleys. The reason why this house was never built is lost; as the design stands it emphasizes a point that has been made particularly in connection with Moor Crag but which reappears in many of the major houses. This is the practice which Voysey developed to such an extent of differentiating the two major elevations by stylistic tricks, particularly related to roof layout. In the Bexhill house the south elevation was to have two double-height bays with a verandah inset between. In an exaggeration of the form used on the lake-front elevation of Broadleys, the roof pitch is brought down and round the bays to form a low roof over the verandah. The same thing happens on the garden front of Moor Crag though without the emphasis of the closely set bays. On the north side of the Bexhill house, by contrast, would have been gables and dormers and a corner tower. The effect is an abrupt contrast between elevations, one low and sweeping, the eye aware of the (in this case) green of the tiles; the other much higher, emphasized by the white of the roughcast on gable and corner tower. It is a distinctive and often repeated stylistic device, though here it shows more emphatically than usual.

31
Design for a house in Collington Avenue,
Bexhill, Sussex, for A.Barker, 1898.
Perspectives of front and rear elevations, with
watercolour, plus plans. Unexecuted.

32
Watercolour perspective executed by Voysey
himself of a house, called Oakhurst, designed
for Mrs E.F.Chester at Fernhurst, Sussex,
1900. The painting is dated 1901 and shows the
house as executed; the foliage details are
typical of Voysey's style.

Spade House

Into 1899, work on the houses at Windermere went on and another unusual and
demanding project began; this was a house to be built at Sandgate, near
Folkestone, for the author H.G.Wells.

In this house also there is an additional interest to tracing the evolution of the
design through several schemes. The major distinction of the design is that it was a
house planned to fit into the differing levels of the site. Voysey designed several
such houses; New Place at Haslemere is an early instance, where the three-storey
bay abuts the terrace at first-floor level. A more consistent example, probably
based upon the work and experiment of the house for H.G.Wells, was the house
for Mrs Chester, called Oakhurst, built at Fernhurst, Sussex and designed in
August 1900. This house (32) is otherwise unimaginative but shows a south terrace
only one storey in height, the main house being set back into the slope below this.
A substantial part of the reasoning behind this stems from an extension of the
comments made above on the liking Voysey had for playing with roof lines.
Oakhurst has all the benefits of a two-storey house, including a two-storey hall;
yet the aspect from the south is of an extremely low, snug, single-storey building.
Another instance where the use of split level accentuates the lowness of the
building while providing adequate accommodation is the cottage for Miss
M.Foster Melliar at Ampthill, Bedfordshire. This house offered living space plus,
for Miss Foster Melliar's work as a nurse or nanny, two bedrooms and a nursery;
in the small building the basement room provided by the slope of the site gave
valuable storage space for, among other things, prams.

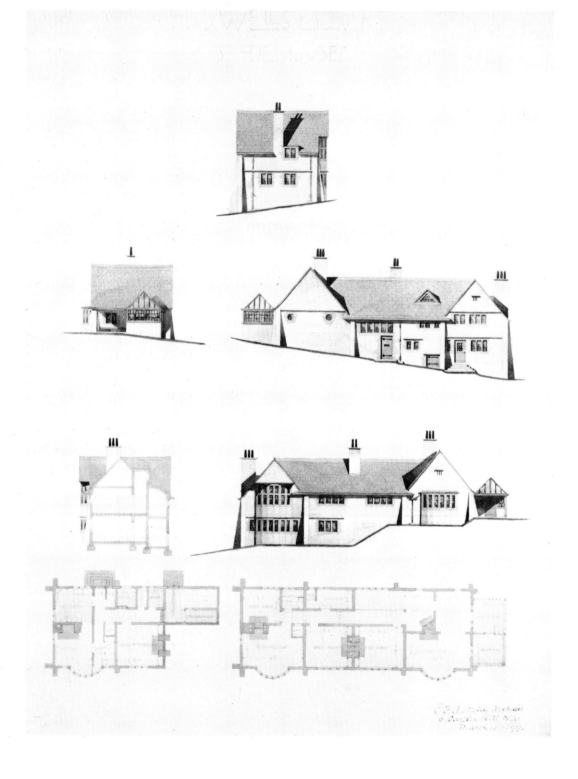

Second scheme for a house, called Spade
House, at Sandgate, Folkestone, Kent, for
H.G.Wells, 1899; elevations, cross-section and
plans. Not executed in this form.

To return to the H.G.Wells house: this again shows the progression of a design through a series of evolving stages before client and architect were satisfied. The first design is dated March 5 1899 – that is, before the final Moor Crag scheme was approved; the main entrance is at the lower level which contains services and accommodation for a servant; a staircase leads up to the main floor with the family living space. On the single-storey elevation is a conservatory. The roof is a pitch roof with two cross gables. Only a week later – March 11 – the second scheme appeared (33a), different only in detail; the gable over the two-storey bay now projects forward over it, the bays are slightly wider and the kitchen size is changed.

The house as built is shown in a third scheme of which a perspective drawing is illustrated (33b). There are considerable changes; the curved bays are gone, two square bays in different positions replacing them. This reflects changes in plan; the dining-room and living-room, formerly at opposite ends of the house with bedrooms between, are now brought together. The living-room is renamed 'the study'. Perhaps Voysey thought that famous authors needed to study, but not to live. This change of layout enables the introduction of a favoured Voysey device, the sheltered verandah between the two main rooms though in this case it is accessible only from the dining-room. In this final scheme the cross gables have gone, the bays have hipped slate roofs and the main roof is also hipped. So, although internally there has not been need for a great deal of change, the split-level form remaining, the effect on the appearance of the house is considerable. One surmises that the reasons behind much of the change were financial – the simplifying of the roof structure, the omission of the conservatory – and certainly the final version of the house has a lot less visual interest than the first. Spade House now stands in considerably altered form; Voysey himself added a further storey in 1903.

In April 1899 Voysey also produced plans and drawings for a project in Devon, the building of a cottage hospital; the building offers capacity for a few patients in the two main wards which form the forward-jutting wings of the building. It is a single-storey building, F-shaped in plan; there is a long, low centre block with a cross gable at each end, which projects to form wings on the south side; the various offices are in the tail of the F. The north (entrance) front has a long verandah, recessed under the eaves. The roof ridges of the cross wings are noticeably higher than that of the central span. The buttresses to the single-storey walls are more than usually emphatic in their reduced height. In plan the layout is simple, a single row of consulting, nurses' and doctor's rooms along the central block; wards in the wings; and all other services in the extension of the centre block (34).

Voysey's relationship with his clients

In a *Studio* article of April 1899 on some of Voysey's recently designed houses the writer mentions comments made by the architect in a previous interview:
> One of Mr Voysey's rare outbursts of temper was directed, while
> I talked to him recently, against those inconsiderate clients who
> endeavoured to insist upon his adding a foot or two to the height of a

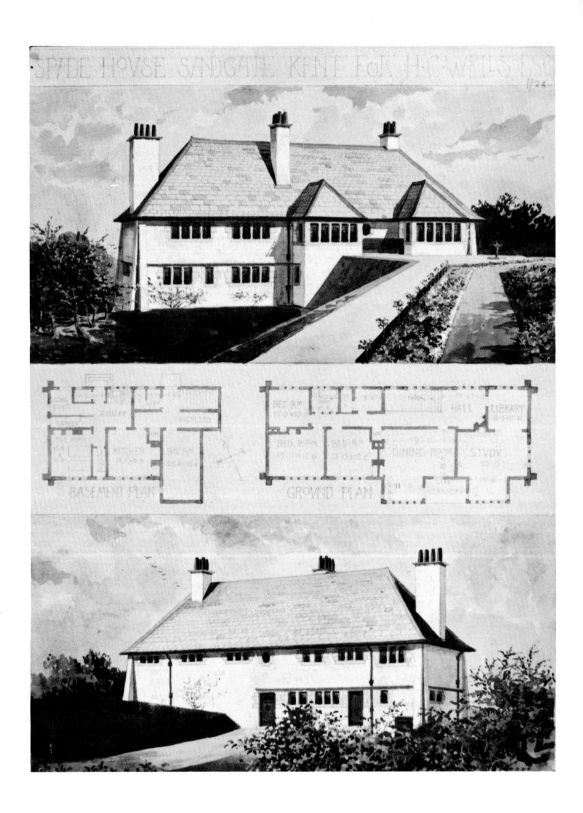

SPADE HOVSE SANDGATE KENT FOR H·C·WELLS ESQ.

BASEMENT PLAN

GROVND PLAN

THE "WINSFORD" COTTAGE HOSPITAL FOR MRS MEDLEY

BEAWORTHY DEVON

C.F.A.VOYSEY ARCHT

MENS WARD 24·0 ×15·0

WOMENS WARD 24·0 ×15·0

ACCIDENT WARD 19·6 × 14·6

CHILDRENS WARD 19·3 × 14·3

BATH RM 9·0 × 7·0

VERANDAH SEAT

6·0 WIDE CORRIDOR

DOWN LOOSE PARA COAL WASH HOUSE SCUL KITCHEN NURSES ROOM LINEN OPERATING HALL SURGERY DRESSERS NURSES
MORTUARY BOX TIN CERY 12·0×12·0 15·6 × 12·0 ROOM ROOM ROOM
10·0 12·0 7·6 WIDE 12·0×12·0 10·6 10·6

33b
Third scheme for the H.G.Wells house, 1899, showing the house almost as executed. Perspectives of front and rear and plans.

34
Design for a Cottage Hospital at Halwill, near Beaworthy, Devon, for Mrs Medley, 1899. Perspectives of front and rear elevations with watercolour and plan, showing the hospital as executed; the building is still in use as a hospital.

second storey, regardless of the fact that by doing this the entire proportion, that is to say, the main beauty, of their house must be sacrificed. It led the designer to digress into an interesting consideration of the relations which ought to exist between client and architect. According to Mr Voysey – and there are few architects who will not agree with him – the client's wishes as regards accommodation, including general scheme of plan, and essentially as regards expense, should be a law to the architects, but the latter should be supreme touching artistic design and proportion.[2]

We do not know which of his houses or clients occasioned the outburst of temper that the *Studio* writer tells us about. It is, however, a useful coincidence that a series of letters survives from this date and gives us a good insight into a matter which would otherwise be a blind spot – the details of a relationship between Voysey and a client. The conclusions we draw from it coincide, more or less, with those the *Studio* has summarized for us but it is the process of its development, and the way in which it is handled, that gives the correspondence its interest.

The client is Cecil, later Sir Cecil, Fitch, a barrister; at the time of the building of his house, Gordondene in Wimbledon, London he was a young man of 29, in the first flush of success, highly intelligent and determined not to be done down, to get exactly what he wanted and not to pay over the odds for it. At the same time – as he tells us in the correspondence – he was not an unreasonable man. Voysey was then in his early forties, well established and busy. His first letter is dated August 21st 1899 and is addressed to 'Mr Fitch'; at Voysey's request the more friendly, 'My dear Fitch' and 'My dear Voysey' are adopted after this first letter, a sure sign that relations were on the whole satisfactory.[3] The stable block of the house is to be a block attached to a corner of the main building by a covered passage; on Oct. 10 1899 Voysey writes:

> I cannot spoil my proportions by cutting off the stable roof. We must manage by moving the stable building five feet to the East and the house five feet to the West and three or four feet to the South. You won't mind that, will you? ... As to the light in the hall I hope you will forgive me for saying you know nothing about it at all. You will ruin the look of the hall from the outside and the in if you alter the staircase window, which is going to light the hall magnificently.[4]

The subject of light into rooms was one which had exercised Voysey when he was being interviewed for the *Studio* article quoted above so it was clearly one which was much on his mind – we might infer, one about which his clients, in view of the apparent smallness of the windows in his houses, gave him some trouble:

> I may say in passing that Mr Voysey characterizes himself as a 'stickler for light', though, by those who lend a mere surface consideration to his work, he is often found fault with for the smallness of his windows. He points out, however, that such critics do not take into consideration the size and height of the rooms these long low windows are intended to give light to. In proportion to a lofty room a low room, he avers, needs much less window space ... In a low room the entire ceiling acts as a reflector and throws the light downwards into every corner of the interior.[5]

In the light of these comments, Mr Fitch's reply to Voysey is interesting; written on Oct. 11, it demonstrates that the client is taking a keen interest in what goes on:

> As regards the light in the hall you are no doubt correct in saying I know nothing about it and if you say there is sufficient I am more than satisfied.
>
> As regards the movement of the stables you will recollect your statement that to move the house further downhill would enormously increase the cost. It was because of this statement of yours that I altered

in the plan the position of the main body of the house in relation to the part containing the dining room and kitchen. I moved the latter portion downhill to give room for the passage to the yard and left the main portion where it was. You now seem to propose to move the whole house bodily downhill (i.e. five feet to the West and three or four feet to the South). If you assure me now that it will not increase the cost of the house I don't mind but if it will I mind very much when I see that two feet off the length of a gable will obviate the difficulty. Seriously, do you think the difference of that two feet will spoil the proportion of the stable roof? I tried it and did not think it would, but you know best and I don't desire to be in any way unreasonable. Perhaps some other way may be found so long as it adds nothing to the expense.[6]

The careful and legal mind of Fitch has put the architect very much on the spot and in his reply the architect has to fight for his dignity and to justify his points – indeed, he gives in over the hall windows, perhaps in order to carry his larger point over the siting of the buildings; his reply again is very quick, written on October 12, the day after Fitch's:

Many thanks for your most reasonable letter. You make me quite ashamed of my own impulsive and strong language. I wish to be emphatic but not rude. I will look to your light. Certainly bringing the building very much forward would increase the cost, but if we bring it only three feet to the South and five feet to the West I think the extra cost will be small because the ground does not drop so much in the West corner. Then we can compromise by cutting off a little from the stable roof and shifting the stabling perhaps a trifle. Room must be made somehow for turning a carriage, that is essential.[7]

The exact details of the dispute and negotiation are not, for the present purpose, very important; what is, is to see the process of attack, clearly natural to him, in which Voysey engaged. In Fitch he seems to have met a strong opponent. It is apparent that a client who approached Voysey knew to some extent what he was going to get: a roughcast house with stone facings and iron casements, in a very modern idiom and built to a very high standard. He would also have to accept that the whole house and its fittings would be designed to the same exacting and austere standard. Fitch clearly rebelled here, his expressed excuse being the need for economy though one suspects that this was a sop to Voysey to disguise the need for a greater show of luxury than Voysey's spartan and excellently crafted fittings would afford. So, when the project for this house was a good deal further on and the plumbing and fittings were being installed, Voysey writes from the heart on 4 Feb. 1901:

I am distressed to see the appallingly ugly and gaudy lavatory and bath that have been sent down and to hear that there is to be no casing in so that the very 'ornamental' brackets will be a veritable cobweb to catch the dust and dirt. No human creature can ever keep them clean. I had provided beautiful clean oak casing that would have looked gentlemanly and dignified.[8]

35a
The Orchard, Voysey's own house at Chorleywood, Hertfordshire, 1899; the garden front.

The correspondence continues in this vein on Feb. 14:

> You have altered all the plumbing and I have no idea what the fittings will be like. I don't think any client deserves to save anything if he makes alterations. I really cannot pity you.[8]

And by March 25 Voysey sounds a little strained and belligerent; he does retain, as he has throughout, a sense of humour which is expressed in the light irony of some of his comments so he is clearly not too angry with Fitch:

> ... I think you ought to pay me some compensation in addition as it involves my doing what to any professional eye would be considered a gross blunder ... the wilful planning of a huge dust trap. Surely it is very hard to be expected to do such a thing against all one's instincts of fitness and good manners ... You must really wait until my work is finished before you criticize it. Then if you don't like it you can pull it down.[8]

In a last letter of 9 May, also 1901, Voysey writes:

> The greatest help will be for you to make up your mind that you cannot have first class material and workmanship without going to a first class builder and paying a first class price.[8]

Gordondene is now demolished. It is fitting that the only Voysey house to be pulled down, particularly a substantial one from the best years of his work, has left us at least this partial record of the process of its building. Voysey was not, as this

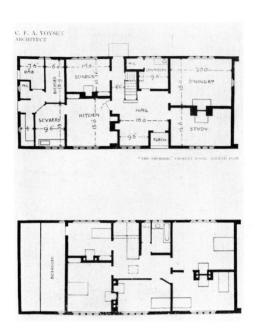

C. F. A. VOYSEY
ARCHITECT

35b
The Orchard, ground- and first-floor plans.

correspondence tells us, the easiest man to work with and when questions of taste and the aesthetic of his work were concerned he stuck to his guns. On other matters – and remembering his own judgement, quoted at the beginning of this section, as to what belonged correctly to the architect to decide, and what to the client – he was open to argument and to persuasion and retained a sense of proportion and of humour in the process. If the above extracts show us no more than that about his methods of working, then they are worth the effort of study.

From 1900 to 1905:

The first five years of the present century continued as an extremely busy period for Voysey in which several fine houses were built: there was The Orchard, Voysey's own house, for which the design was begun in 1899 and carried through into 1900; The Pastures in 1901; Vodin in 1902; Higham in 1904; and the factory for Sandersons in 1902 and the Whitwood Institute in 1904. If for no other reason than its unexpectedness – though in fact it is a house of interest – one includes finally the house built at Aswan in Egypt in 1905. In addition to these there are various smaller and lesser houses, each of which has its own particular points of interest.

The Orchard

The Orchard, strictly speaking, should be spoken of as a house of 1899 since the dating given in this account is throughout the date of first design, not of completion. However, as the best example of the type of smaller house – for it is considerably smaller than most of the other houses referred to in this chapter – The Orchard fits more happily into the account at this point. The Orchard was built at Chorleywood, north-west of London and within easy commuting distance; it is appropriate that since the domestic architecture of the years around the turn of the century was above all the architecture of the new suburbs, of the comfortable, detached and medium-sized house, Voysey should have chosen to locate his house here. One suspects that it was a decision made to fulfil family needs rather than expressing personal preference to be outside the metropolis. The house itself (35a) adopts a form Voysey has shown already a liking for, a hipped roof with cross gables at each end over a rectangular form; here, though, the rectangle is unadorned by porches, verandahs, bays, dormers or any of the usual trimmings of a Voysey house. Only at the east end is a lean-to which allows the roof pitch over it – as at Moor Crag which has the same roof form – to run down to first-floor level. In plan (35b) the recessed porch is seen to give onto a corner of the hall; diagonally opposite, by the garden entrance, are the stairs. The width of the hall separates dining-room and study from the schoolroom, though one cannot imagine that Voysey children would have been encouraged to be noisy children. Services are also grouped at this end, away from the main living rooms. Upstairs a simple arrangement of bedrooms and bathrooms opening from a central landing offers maximum use of the space available. The distinction of the house lay in its interior finishings and furniture, where Voysey was free to exercise his wishes (see below,

36a
Contemporary photograph of The Pastures,
North Luffenham, Rutland, for Miss
G.Conant, 1901. The garden fronts.

36b
Contemporary photograph of The Pastures,
the entrance courtyard and stable wing; just
visible behind and to the left of the tree is the
bell-tower.

chapter 5); downstairs the hall and service rooms are paved with grey slates; upstairs are green cork tiles. The woodwork was painted deal – it would be interesting to know whether it was budget or choice that decided him against his favourite oak, untreated. One suspects the former. The bright red curtains which appear in Voysey's coloured elevations of many of his houses were actually fitted here, as were one or two of the quieter of his own wallpapers. The furniture was almost entirely to his own designs.

Country Life published a short description of Voysey's own house while it was still under construction, commenting:

> This pleasant little house ... is growing into shape, or by this time has grown into it, at Chorleywood, in the sylvan countryside of Herts ... Its situation is as nearly ideal as may be ... Its cost is to be between £1000 and £1500, and, speaking frankly, we do not see what more can be desired by any man of moderate means whose quiver is not very full indeed ... Hot and cold water is laid on everywhere, for the pleasing air of rusticity in this house, studied as it is in reality goes hand in hand with a nice appreciation of creature comforts.[9]

The Pastures, Sandersons and Vodin

Many of Voysey's houses are clustered together in small areas; the Surrey houses, the Lake District houses, the Malvern houses. The Pastures at North Luffenham in what was, until recently, the small county of Rutland, stands on its own. The client was Miss G. Conant whose family was long established in a village nearby. The house is on the edge of the old village of North Luffenham, looking out across open fields. As can be seen from two contemporary photographs (36a and b) the house is built round a courtyard with one side open. The house and services occupy two sides, the third being a single-storey wing of stables. The south and west fronts opening onto the garden are distinguished by a series of gables; the two main gables have two-storey bay windows, the subsidiary ones are to dormers, the detailed treatment differing on the two fronts. A large semi-circular opening on the south front provides a sheltered verandah and leads to the garden entrance. The dominant feature of the courtyard elevations is a bell tower.

It is understood that Voysey wished The Pastures to be built in local stone – just as he had originally wished for Broadleys; it seems though that the family, both for reasons of cost and of appearance, preferred the roughcast finish. Overruled in this matter, Voysey had the consolation of laying out the gardens to the house himself.

1902 saw the design of Voysey's most distinctive building which, paradoxically, was one of very few not intended for domestic use and his only industrial building. The factory (37) provided additional space for Sandersons, the wallpaper manufacturer for whom Voysey produced many designs, next to their existing factory at Chiswick. The bridge shown on the perspective drawing, linking the two factories, was not built. The white finish was achieved with glazed brick, banded with dark blue brick and stone coping. The remarkable appearance of the building calls to mind the structure of a piece of Voysey's furniture – the

Messrs. A Sanderson & Sons New Factory at Chiswick.

C.F.A. Voysey
Architect
London

37
Perspective watercolour of the Sandersons
factory at Chiswick, 1902.

capped supporting piers, the curvilinear coping – and suggests that Voysey's aim
was to drop a 'box' for the production of wallpapers down into London's suburbs.
It is very difficult to appreciate the building for it is hemmed in by others; it must
be recognized, though, that this was also true when it was built and may help to
explain the singular dominance of the roof-line.

As his style matured Voysey developed to a finer and finer art the skill of
making a greater simplicity look more achieved; nowhere is this truer than in the
house called Vodin, also designed in 1902. Approaching along the main drive,
the house, situated at Pyrford Common just south of London, gives a strong

impression of substantiality; and yet its form is simply rectangular with a hipped roof. The only relief on the entrance front comes from the porch and the staircase tower, on the garden front from the arched door opening followed by the line of the drip course. There are none of the usual stylistic tricks played with the roof, no dormers, cross gables, low eaves. The elevations (38a and b) are an exercise in simplicity and much of the effect comes solely from the arrangement of fenestration and the sparse use of curve (38c). In the first scheme for the house, the drawing dated August 1902, the porch which is now such a dominant feature was pencilled in with the note, 'may be omitted' and the staircase tower did not appear in this scheme, so the house only narrowly escaped being very plain indeed. The house also has a cluster of service buildings, coach-house and cottage, single-storey, facing the front entrance (38d).

Already, with the completion of the Sandersons building and Vodin, there is a distinct feeling that the height of Voysey's career was past; some notable buildings were yet to come but the pace was slowing. Voysey always produced a number of unexecuted designs, as do most architects. There is no reason to think that his projects, when they failed to go ahead, were the victims of disagreement between architect and client. 1903, though, saw the failure of a commission from one of his best clients, W. Ward Higgs, who on this occasion commissioned a town house to be built at Bognor. He had moved his family here from the house Voysey had earlier fitted out for him in Queensborough Terrace in London. For this new design Voysey reverted to the 'Tower House' form for which he had shown favour in his very early years. The house, though, was not built. Nor was a design of 1904 for a house in Hampstead; also in 1904, there was an unsuccessful competition entry for a Library and Museum at Limerick. The houses that were built at this period were slight: the White Cottage, Wandsworth, for C.T. Coggin, begun in 1903; a small convalescent home for children at Bushey, Herts, begun in 1904, called Myholme; and, most effective of this group, a small house also for Miss E. Somers, the client of Myholme, situated quite close to her nursing home and begun in the same year (39). This small house, called Tilehurst, has a good example of the prominent, flat-roofed porch which Voysey seemed to favour for houses of this size (cf. Littleholme in Kendal for A.W. Simpson, see 45).

Higham and the Whitwood Institute

There was a paradox in Voysey's character and work. The man who was instrumental in reconciling thoroughgoing middle-class respectability with a modesty in domestic surrounding that would a few years before his work have been unthinkable, was also himself a quite fearful, though quite unmalicious, snob. The best practical instance of the workings of this paradox occurs in 1904 and alleviates the year's otherwise drabness in building and design. It concerns two projects, both of which will be illustrated here by the architect's drawings rather than by photographs of the finished buildings, even though both projects were completed. The particular reason for this is that neither was completed under the architect's own supervision. The first, a house at Higham, Woodford, Essex, for Lady Henry Somerset, came to construction by 1906 but did so without the

38a
Vodin at Pyrford Common near Woking for
F. Walters, 1903; the entrance front.

38b
Vodin, the garden front.

38c
Vodin, a detail of the entrance porch.

38d
Vodin, the lodge and outbuildings.

39
Tilehurst, Bushey, Hertfordshire, for Miss
E.Somers, 1904; the front and side elevations.

40

Design for a house at Higham, Woodford,
Essex, for Lady Henry Somerset, 1904;
watercolour perspectives of front and rear
elevations plus plans.

supervision which Voysey would, of course, have given to the job himself if he
and his client had been on good terms. The only similar case is Dixcot, on Tooting
Common, where following various disagreements the house was in fact finished
by Walter Cave. The second was the project for an Institute and housing for
miners at Whitwood, Yorkshire; this has already been mentioned above in the
context of Broadleys for the Whitwood Institute was the brainchild of Currer
Briggs, the client of that house. That project was finished without Voysey's
superintendence because the Company's budget did not permit of it. It is of course
possible, though we cannot know, that Voysey's aristocratic client dispensed with
his supervision for the same reason.

The house that Voysey designed for Lady Henry Somerset (40) is impressive;
the first scheme as shown is undated though other drawings are dated March 1904;

HOVSES·FOR·MESSRS·HY·BRIGGS·&·SON.
AT·WHITWOOD·NORMANTON·YORKSHIRE.
C·F·A·VOYSEY·ARCHITECT·23·YORK·PLACE·W^c
Invtel:delt.

41
Watercolour perspective of the Colliery
Institute and housing at Whitwood, near
Normanton, Yorkshire, for Henry Briggs and
Son and Co., 1904–5. Only one terrace of
houses plus the Institute (the corner building)
were completed, substantially as detailed here.

the second, which incorporates several changes, has the date April 15 1904. The house was to be of stone and arranged on an F-shaped plan, the main body of the house with two projecting wings, to which is added as the tail of the F the service wing. Many of the motifs in the design of the house are familiar and need no special explanation. Two features do, however, stand out: first the massive stone porch, two storeys in height with a lipped parapet slightly ramped in the centre. This feature is reminiscent, and quite deliberately so (note the narrow slit openings beside the clock) of a medieval castle. Second the curvilinear parapet to the front of the 'Winter Garden' roof terrace on the garden side. This evokes the form used on the roof-line of the Sandersons factory; it is rendered and it has a substantially 'Art Nouveau' feel about it though Voysey, who strongly deprecated that movement, would not have admitted to such an influence. It also appears from the perspective that Voysey intended, on the garden front, to render the top segment of the twin gables and the gables to the dormers, thus emphasizing the difference in style between entrance and garden elevations: the former is dignified, formal, massive; the latter domestic, informal, intimate. In plan the house shows the same love of clustering the main rooms round a central hall that we have come to recognize as a feature of Voysey's work. Notable is the inclusion of a chapel which we might regard as pointing further the appearance of a definite medieval influence in the design – the significance of this will be seen better in the chapter on Voysey's later work. The differences between the two schemes mentioned above are not great; in the second the entrance is moved to one end from being centred on the family part of the house; the projecting wings become round-ended, the chapel is moved and the number of bedrooms considerably reduced. Though a stone porch is retained, the rest of the entrance front is roughcast and so much of the medieval feel is lost. The dormers on the garden front disappear. So the second scheme, while clearly in part modified to cut costs, is also considerably de-natured and less emphatic in style. As built, the house differed considerably from both the schemes considered here.

The Institute and terraced housing for Currer Briggs, for which the first scheme is dated September 14 1904, is an interesting contribution to the garden suburb idea and to the tradition of the benevolent employer. The notion of the garden city and its stablemate, the garden suburb, was in the air at the turn of the century and Bournville, Letchworth, Port Sunlight and Hampstead were talking points among those concerned with housing and design standards. A Garden City Association was formed including members as diverse as Earl Grey, Walter Crane and Bernard Shaw. The ideals involved could give rise to excesses of well-meaning enthusiasm:

> The scheme [i.e. Bournville] shows what is possible by well-conceived private enterprise, and we believe the lesson will not be lost upon a country which still produces the philosopher and the poet. For such a scheme is built with broad bases on the living rock, and shall be hereafter amongst those things which remain.[10]

Yet they were sound and humane, and above all practicable, in an age which had gone beyond the first phases of unthinking industrialization and required a more sophisticated social machinery to cope with the problems of accommodating its workforces. There is, in keeping with the mood of those years, a certain sense of

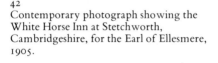

42
Contemporary photograph showing the White Horse Inn at Stetchworth, Cambridgeshire, for the Earl of Ellesmere, 1905.

43
Hollymount, Knotty Green, Buckinghamshire, for C.T.Burke, designed in 1905 and completed, as the tablet over the door records, in 1907; the elevation to the street.

44
Contemporary photograph of The Homestead, Frinton-on-Sea, Essex, for S.C.Turner, 1905–6; the entrance front.

feudalism or benevolent despotism about the whole matter but since this reflected a reality, though one that was about to change, it was inevitable. Certainly this feel of medievalism may have been instrumental in exciting Voysey to contribute to the garden suburb movement, in quite a minor way, with his Institute and workmen's cottages for Currer Briggs. In fact only one terrace of houses were built with the Institute itself, Currer Briggs finding, as noted above, that philanthropy on this scale became expensive for a poor colliery owner.

The scheme is designed in roughcast with red tiles, the stone dressings of the design giving way to wooden window frames with no leading in the construction. The whole design (41) is harmonious with a pleasant regularity of gable and dormer along the terrace. The feature of the design, the square tower of the Institute with its vestigial crenellations and sparse fenestration, echoes quite surprisingly the porch of Lady Somerset's house in London and emphasizes the emergence in Voysey's work of a preoccupation with medieval form.

The close of the decade, 1905–9

These closing years of the busiest and best part of Voysey's career saw the continuance of the trend indicated above, away from the major commissions towards smaller houses and fewer. In 1905 the White Horse Inn at Stetchworth was designed for the Earl of Ellesmere and progressed through to a seventh revised

45a
Design for Lodge Style at Combe Down, near Bath, for T.Sturge Cotterell, 1909; the first scheme. Not executed in this form.

plan before the aristocratic client was satisfied with it (42). Also begun at the time were Hollymount at Knotty Green, near Beaconsfield (designed 1905–6) and The Homestead at Frinton-on-Sea (designed 1905–6), both of which were successful though quite small houses (43 and 44). Since each was also fitted out by Voysey with furnished interiors these will be dealt with in more detail in chapter 5 which concerns his interior design work. 1906–7 also produced the design and furnishing of the interior of Garden Corner in Chelsea for E.J.Horniman, one of Voysey's principal clients; this too will be dealt with in that later chapter. One of the most unusual commissions also came at this time, though regrettably the details are lost as to how. For Dr H.E.Leigh Canney Voysey designed a house to be built – and it was – at Aswan in Egypt. It also was in roughcast with dressings of local sandstone. The drawings, dated from Sept. to Oct. 1905, show quite a complex plan form

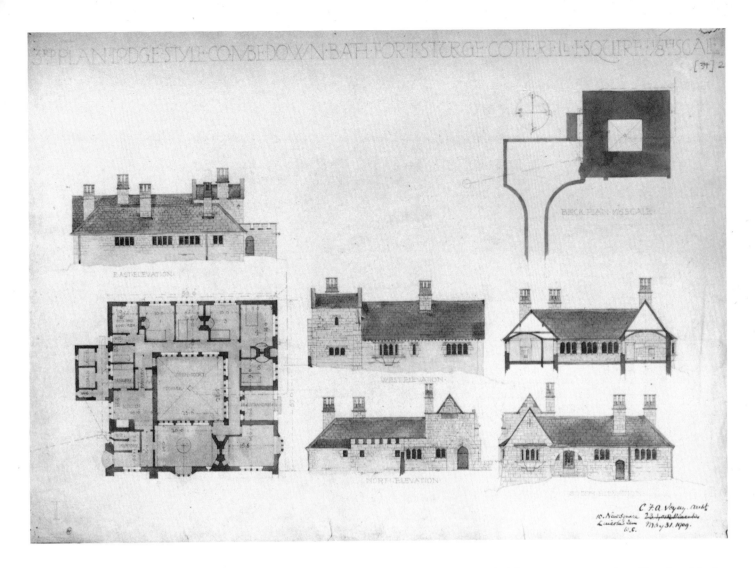

3RD·PLAN·LODGE·STYLE·COMBE DOWN·BATH·FOR T S TORGE COTTEREIL ESQUIRE·1/8TH·SCALE

45b
Design for Lodge Style, the third scheme, showing the house as executed.

with a terrace built up on two sides and elaborate arrangement of levels with the single-storey hall and drawing-room on a mezzanine with bedrooms and services below and bedrooms and dining-room above. There is also a crenellated parapet. Voysey did not supervise the construction.

Then, at the end of the decade, came a spate of commissions for small houses each of a distinct interest; Lodge Style at Combe Down near Bath; Littleholme at Kendal; a house at Brooke End, Henley-in-Arden; and an unexecuted project for a house for the Hampstead Garden Suburb Development Company.

Lodge Style was built for T.S.Cotterell and was an eccentric commission which fell in very well with Voysey's inclinations at that time. The story goes that the client wanted a house reminiscent of Merton College, Oxford built in stone from his own quarry – he was a quarry owner. Voysey produced for him a scheme best

101

45c
Lodge Style, the west elevation.

described as Collegiate Bungalow style, to be built around a courtyard or, more properly in this case, quadrangle, forty feet by thirty feet. There was a pitched, gabled roof; the entrance and windows were thoroughly Gothic in detail, with oriels on the west and north elevations, pointed arch windows with narrow lights on the others and a crenellated extension on the entrance front (45a). The scheme, unhappily, was whittled down so that as built (45b and c) the quadrangle has become a cramped 23 feet by 21 feet (approximately), though pointed windows and entrance, crenellations and oriels do survive in a modified form. Inside are stone fireplaces and other detailing appropriate to the Gothic exterior. It is an intriguing, but not altogether attractive or successful, scheme.

As different as can be is Littleholme, built at Kendal for Voysey's friend and colleague A.W.Simpson, furniture maker and designer. The only point of similarity is that both houses, unusually, are in stone. Littleholme has an enormous porch (46a), a simple, flat structure with massive wooden beam supports, which contrasts with the plain, forthright appearance of the house (46b). In plan the bulk of the ground-floor space is given over to a large, L-shaped sitting-room with a deep ingle-nook. In its original form the house was furnished largely with furniture, not to Voysey's designs but to Simpson's own. About 1923 Voysey designed a crenellated extension for the house but this was never built.

46a
Littleholme, Kendal, for A.W.Simpson, 1909;
the entrance porch.

46b
Littleholme, the house from Sedbergh Road.

47a
Brooke End, Henley-in-Arden,
Warwickshire, for Miss F.Knight, 1909; the
entrance front showing the attenuated porch
in brick with stone dressings.

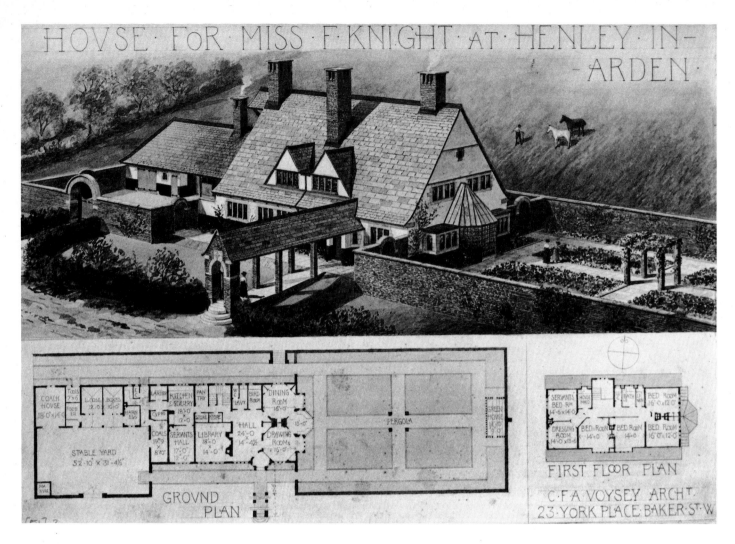

HOVSE · FOR · MISS · F · KNIGHT · AT · HENLEY · IN-
-ARDEN ·

GROVND PLAN

FIRST FLOOR PLAN

C · F · A · VOYSEY · ARCHT
23 · YORK · PLACE · BAKER · ST · W

47b
Design for Brooke End; perspective
watercolour with plans showing the house as
built except for the length of the porch.

If Lodge Style represents the way Voysey's mind, given only the slightest encouragement, was beginning to run towards a heavily mannered blend of his own style with neo-Gothic, and Littleholme the whittling down of his life-long ideals of plainness and good workmanship, then the house at Brooke End, Henley-in-Arden shows how, given a straightforward client, these two facets of his style and personality might resolve themselves. It is (47a) a conventional small Voysey house, though with some unconventional plan details, including octagonal rooms and a prominent conservatory(47b). The unusual feature is a long, projecting porch (though not, in the finished house, as long as the drawing would suggest) with pitched roof, a pointed arch opening and stone dressings. The flavour of this is undeniably Gothic and its contrast with the rest of the house emphasized by the use of exposed brickwork rather than a rendered finish. To round off this eccentric year, 1909, is a design which unfortunately was not executed. This the drawing announces as, 'Proposed House for the Hampstead Garden Suburb Development Company, Hampstead. Plot no.338 in Bigwood Road for Miss Lang'. Like Littleholme it was to have a simple rectangular form, though here the more usual roughcast finish was to have been used. The house is set sideways to the road; there is a very steeply pitched roof with gables and into each roof slope a hipped dormer with wooden frames is fitted. The drawing is dated 6 Sept. 1909. It is unusual that Voysey, the champion and one of the few fully accomplished practitioners of the new vernacular style of domestic architecture, was not asked to take part in at least one of the mass housing projects which were becoming prevalent at this time. Perhaps his reputation for difficulty prevented such approaches; perhaps they were made and rejected; here, certainly, something intervened to prevent the house being built, so unfortunately Voysey remains one of the few distinguished domestic architects of his day not to be represented in the important work of the building of the Hampstead Garden Suburb.

In arriving at the end of this first decade of the present century we have followed through those years of hectic practice when Voysey produced the bulk of his best work; from the picturesque accomplishment of Moor Crag, the homely stateliness of Broadleys, through the consistently changing themes and moods, all to a basically similar plan, of Spade House, The Orchard, The Pastures, Vodin, to the diminution – in form though not in skill – of these four houses of 1909; en route, the graceful eccentricity of the Sandersons factory, the venture into social theory of the Whitwood Institute, the sheer oddity of the house at Aswan. The scene now must change, before we return to a consideration of the long but relatively empty years of the end of Voysey's life and work, to consideration of what went on inside some of the many houses where Voysey was allowed to influence the design and furnishing of his building. So first we look at the furniture which his mature years produced, then at some of the specific interiors he designed.

Chapter 5 Furniture Designs, 1898–1910 and the Voysey Interior

A mean man will inevitably tend to shabbiness in the hidden parts of his work; he will put deal bottoms to his satinwood casket, and fasten up his joinery with screws or nails to save the labour of dovetailing or mortising. How often we see effectiveness in the place of genuine quality. What looks rich but is only brainless elaboration. An anxiety to appear clever rather than to be clever, to make a show to create applause and attract attention, are all due to love of self more than love of virtue for its own sake.[1]

Voysey had two principal concerns in designing the furniture to be used in his houses and he sums them up in this statement: first to produce a design which eschews 'brainless elaboration', that is to say which adopts the minimum of stylistic trickery and ornament consistent with usefulness and appearance; second to seek, not 'effectiveness' but 'genuine quality', to ensure that the work produced is made to a high standard of craftsmanship. The third clue which he offers to his general philosophy of working is the link he so clearly draws between the attainment of the ideal of well-designed craftsmanship and the satisfying of a moral imperative, the search for 'virtue for its own sake'. If we tend to forget that Voysey was both a devout Christian and a committed and consistent moralist, such statements – and they are frequent in his writings – will remind us of it.

It is almost uncanny to see the way in which Voysey's output in 1898 and 1899 suddenly rose to a frenzied rate; the houses of those years we have already seen but their planning did not leave him without the time to produce some of his best-known furniture – and his best – in that brief period. Two chairs from 1898, both widely seen in his interiors (48 and 49), use a similar seat and support structure and an exaggeratedly high back. One incorporates the heart motif which has become a Voysey trademark; a single broad splat is pierced by two hearts, one inverted, the splat being formed to follow and emphasize their shape. The second has a back formed simply of five slats or lathes, arranged vertically. Both chairs are in oak, Voysey's favourite wood. The legs are tapered and chamfer gradually from a square to an octagonal section; this also is a Voysey trademark which will in future be referred to simply as the 'chamfered leg'. The stretchers are plain, rectangular in section and slender; the seat frame is similarly simple with only a curved moulding to relieve the front lower edge. The back supports taper almost to a point and continue some inches above the top rail, exaggerating further the attenuated

48
Dining chair with rush seat, 1898.

49
Contemporary photograph of a dining chair
with arms and a rush seat, 1898.

50
The Kelmscott cabinet, 1899.

effect. The seats are of rush though a leather finish, natural in colour fixed with
close set round-headed bronze tacks, was sometimes used instead. The finish was
clean from the plane, no wax, varnish or stain being used – another Voysey
trademark. If this was the typical Voysey chair from these years, 1898 also
produced the standard cabinet design, later repeated in several slightly differing
forms; it will pay to look at this as closely as the chairs since it also establishes
several recurring features and principles. The example shown (50) is the Kelmscott
cabinet of 1899, unusual in the degree of brass ornament used but differing only in
proportion from the first known use of this form, which was for a music cabinet.
Both pieces, as indeed very probably the first examples of the two chairs, were
produced for one of Voysey's best clients. W. Ward Higgs. At this date Voysey
was preparing for him an interior at 23 Queensborough Terrace, Bayswater in
London. The carcase of the cabinet sits on a wider frame with four tapering legs,
plain stretchers and a simple moulding to the bottom edge. A simple moulding
joins frame to carcase. There are two doors with long strap hinges terminating in
heart shapes – in this case the hearts are incised with bird shapes. The piece is
capped with a heavily overhanging moulded cornice rail, slightly wider than the
bottom frame and with a plain flat top. It is not large – few of Voysey's pieces were
– its overall height being only 133 cm. The original finish would as usual have been
white oak with no dressing, the brass detail left unpolished, though as with most

extant pieces a polish has subsequently been applied. In this case, because the cabinet was made to house an edition of the Kelmscott Press Chaucer, brass plates are attached incised with the words, 'Kelmscott Chaucer'; these plates are laid on red leather which emphasizes the lettering and a contemporary account also refers to a 'vermilion enamelled interior', though no trace of this remains. This piece was unique though several cabinets of similar form and construction were made.

Other pieces were also produced at this period. One was a magnificent dresser (51), an adaptation of the traditional form of such pieces, first made between 1898 and 1900 and later repeated; as with the cabinet there were several known similar designs, including one for H.G.Wells at Spade House. The square supports have square caps to them and another typical feature – seen also in the double bed dealt with earlier – is the carrying up of the supports above the finished height of the piece. The same square, capped supports, carried up over the main structure, are seen in the writing desk or bureau of 1899 (53). This has a fall front with vertical strap hinges, a glazed cupboard below and recessed glazed cupboard above. It is tall, at 219cm only 10cm shorter than the dresser, its height emphasized by a width of only 60cm. Both pieces were in the first instance made for the same client as the Kelmscott cabinet, Ward Higgs; the bureau also was probably later repeated, a design existing for a wider version differing only in detail.

At the end of the decade Voysey was certainly employed in making furniture for his own house, The Orchard. Some pieces used in the house – for example the bed and chest of drawers and the hand-painted clock mentioned in an earlier chapter – were moved from earlier homes but much was specially made, including a cabinet of the Kelmscott type, a wash-stand, a plain wardrobe and various chairs. The interiors of The Orchard will be dealt with and illustrated later.

The use and re-use of basic designs was not unique to Voysey but the consistency with which he did, throughout his career, tend to alter existing forms to new needs is marked. It is largely explained by the importance of proportion in his work and his view that a difference of proportion gave new characteristics to a shape that was similar to another. He writes:

> The sense of proportion being one of temperament far more than
> learning and education, one of feeling far more than thought, will, if
> sincerely exercised, stamp any work of art with the character that is the
> unique possession of its owner. It should be a spontaneous expression
> and never deliberately formularised. When a designer consciously fixes
> a scale of proportion for his own use it becomes a mannerism and
> eccentricity, appearing like self-advertisement, when all the while it
> should be as unnoticed in its birth as our own voices are to ourselves.
> Or when proportions are borrowed, all personal quality is hidden and
> the work strikes us as commonplace and without life, interest or
> distinction. The mathematicians' maxims of Greek proportion leave us
> starved and cold, as if in the presence of death.[2]

This was written considerably later in Voysey's life, in *Individuality* published in 1915, but it is a fair representation of the view he had held for most of his working career.

To speak of the importance of proportion in design is to say everything yet to

say nothing; it is on a par with saying that the ability to write is an important quality for an author to possess – the importance lies in the author's individual awareness of language and the use he makes of whatever special gift or aptitude he may have. The gift itself is a much more personal matter, rarely susceptible of definition; so Voysey's gift for the manipulation of proportion was one of the principal keys to his success as an architect and designer. We see it best in comparing pieces of his work. The dining chair of 1902, for instance (52), is basically the same chair as the lathe-back chair of 1898. It differs in the decorative detail of the back which here is a single broad splat, a single sheet of oak, keyed with exposed dovetails into the back rails and incised with a single heart; it has the same form and structure, the chamfered legs, tapering rear supports, simple decorative curve detail to top and bottom rails, plain stretchers and a choice of seat covering. The proportions are as different as can be – the chair here is broader, lower, the relationship of all its parts to each other changed. It retains absolutely the 'personal quality' which Voysey speaks of above, for the proportions and details he has given it are his own; so does its earlier fellow. Here, in the use of proportion in this way, lies the key to and the demonstration of Voysey's designs; here also lies the explanation of the apparent similarity between many of his designs; the possibility that the critic might turn round and complain of a lack of range is answered by the question, range of what? Voysey chose not to evolve hosts of differing shapes and forms – it is quite beyond doubt that he could have done so had he wished. He chose instead to deal with fineness of proportion.

This single-heart chair subsequently appeared in a range of sizes, some fine, lightweight and delicate, some heavy and chunky; it went into a limited form of production made by F.C.Nielsen; the design was also adapted for production and sale at Liberty's. The latest manifestation of a variation on this range of chairs, the double-heart back, the lathe back and the single-heart back was a chair of 1907 made for the Essex and Suffolk Equitable Insurance Company for use as office furniture.

As has been said earlier, Voysey's favoured material was oak with no finishing treatment of polish or varnish, in conjunction with metal fittings, brass or bronze, which were allowed to dull naturally. The exceptions to this use of materials are few: a mirror frame of 1901 design was 'to be carved in hard wood and gilded [this piece can be seen in the background of 59]; the grain of the wood is not to be filled up'; a clock case, undated on the drawing but made between 1903 and 1906, was in ebony and the drawing notes, 'figures and minutes inlaid with ivory. The whole case to be ebony. Ivory pins for mortices'. The other interesting departure from oak lay in the very few pieces of upholstered furniture. These we know to have been made up for there are contemporary photographs, though no examples survive. An easy chair, first drawing dated Feb. 1900 (54), existed in a number of coverings and with differing arm detail. The frame is oak and much of it is left exposed, the padding being added at strategic points. The structure of the chair resembles that of the dining chairs. Totally different in idea is the tub chair of 1902 (55), high-backed with ribbed padding and upholstery, the back flaring out distinctively at the top. There is no precedent for this in Voysey's work, and no successor. The covering material is not known though it certainly was not one of

52
Dining chair with arms and leather seat, c.1902.

53
Bureau with a fall-front writing desk and glazed cupboards, 1899.

54
Contemporary photograph of an easy chair with dark velvet upholstery, 1900.

55
Contemporary photograph of a tub chair, upholstered, 1902.

56a
Contemporary photograph of a folding table made without metal fixings, 1907.

his own patterned fabrics! It is the only instance of a piece which was upholstered, the timber carcase being completely hidden.

Working on into the first decade of this century Voysey seemed to develop a distinct taste for furniture made without the use of metal. Two such pieces are known and more than one instance of each is known though none appears to survive. Both are tables; the first of Dec. 1903 (this can be seen in 60) has noted on the drawing, 'Oak table, no nails or screws to be used in construction'. The second, of May 1907 (56a), has the note, 'Circular folding table to be made in oak entirely without metal of any kind'. Both tables adopt the principle of supports radiating from a central wooden boss though the folding table – a kind of gateleg with two fixed and four hinged legs – is of far greater constructional complexity as the drawing (56b) shows. The client for this was E.J.Horniman and it was used, as contemporary photographs show, in Garden Corner (see 63). One should also note here that Voysey's earliest furniture design, the Swan chair (see 10), relied in its construction on pinning and pegging with wood alone. It is also generally true that Voysey relied no more heavily on conventional metal fixings in his furniture than he had to; he tended to favour the dowel pin and the use of carefully made joints fixed with glue rather than the quicker and cheaper possible alternatives which metal could have provided but which would have been quite foreign to his notion of what was proper.

One last piece in the survey of the furniture of these years is an oddity, but too distinctive not to mention. Like many of the above it was made up and more than one instance is known; there are photographs but no example survives. The piece is a Chesterfield, though this is a slightly fulsome name for the austere bench seat (57) which, in Voysey's view, was to be used without cushioning. The frame is fitted with lathes of oak to form seat and back, the lathes each dovetailed into the supporting rails. The broad flaps each side are supported on fixed quadrant arms. It is a sad comment on the vagaries of taste that one of these Chesterfields is known to have been banished some years after its manufacture to the garden. Its austerity and structure were thought more appropriate there, and there it stayed until it fell to pieces.

By the end of the decade the changes which were becoming evident in Voysey's architectural work began to permeate into his furniture; there was not much made after about 1907 so the change is not so definite or so easy to trace. This will be looked at in chapter 6 but now, having surveyed briefly the type of furniture Voysey chose to make in these most productive years of his career, we turn to those interiors where he was given a free hand to fit and furnish and where evidence survives to show the use he made of these chances.

The Voysey Interior

Voysey had a strong general awareness of what was required of the domestic interior, though his means of achieving what he thought desirable were not conventional. He shared the preoccupation of his day concerning the importance of the family home:

In the category of qualities of general need we should put repose,

56b
Design for a circular folding table, 1907, as
shown in 56a; the design for E.J.Horniman for
use at Garden Corner, Chelsea.

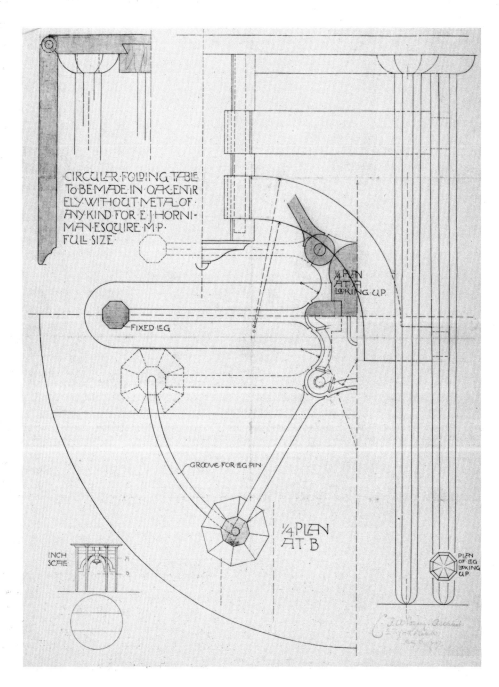

CIRCULER·FOLDING·TABLE
To·BE·MADE·IN·OAK·ENTIR
ELY·WITHOUT·METAL·OF·
ANY·KIND·FOR·E·J·HORNI-
MAN·ESQUIRE·M·P·
FULL·SIZE·

¼ PLAN
AT·A
LOOKING·UP.

FIXED·LEG

GROOVE FOR·LEG·PIN

¼ PLAN
AT·B

INCH
SCALE

PLAN
OF·LEG
LOOKING
UP.

cheerfulness, simplicity, breadth, warmth, quietness in storm, economy
of upkeep, evidence of protection, harmony with surroundings,
absence of dark passages or places, evenness of temperature, making the
home the frame to its inmates, for rich and poor alike will appreciate
these qualities.[3]

This is far more than a practical concern with housing; it is almost a mystique
created about the sanctity of the security and the comfort of life at home, of family
life. As it was a matter on which Voysey, and many of his contemporaries,
whether architects or designers or not, felt deeply, so the failure to achieve the
necessary standard excited strong feeling. Voysey was particularly harsh on the
failure of designers to offer satisfactory domestic surroundings in which an
adequate life could be conducted. He felt strongly outraged when rooms were
crammed with bad furniture or covered in badly designed papers and fabrics; he
deplored the effect this would have on the occupants:

We can produce the sensation of a drunken brawl by our combination
of various coloured articles.[4]

What is more, his standards were high and he often objected on grounds too subtle
for most of us to conceive though we might in retrospect sympathize and agree:

The disturbance of the senses is often very subtle. You go to call on a
friend; you leave the York stone pavement and stand on mosaic or
tiles, then on cocoanut mat, then, possibly, on polished wood and then

57
Contemporary photograph of a Chesterfield,
c.1907.

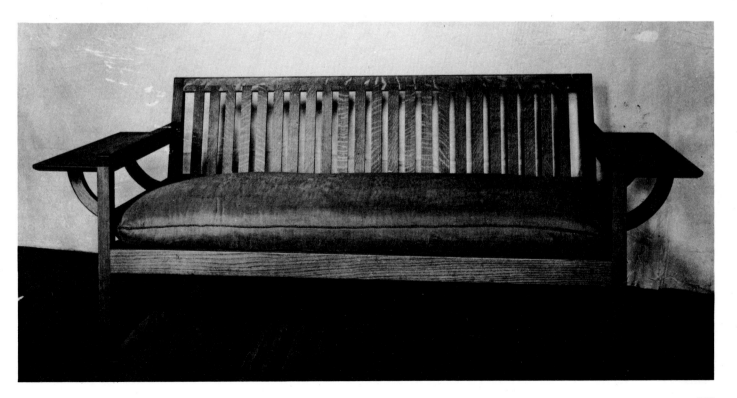

on pile carpet; all varying sensations in rapid succession, which are more or less destructive of repose according to the sensitiveness of the visitor.[4]

The resolution of the problem is, at least in outline, quite simple:

> We cannot be too simple ... we are too apt to furnish our rooms as if we regarded our wallpapers, furniture and fabrics as far more attractive than our friends.[6]

The principal buildings in which Voysey had more or less a free hand to construct a finished interior are 23 Queensborough Terrace (1898–9); his own house, The Orchard (1899); Hollymount, near Beaconsfield (1905–6); The Homestead at Frinton (1905–6); Garden Corner in Chelsea (1906). These are the main ones, all well documented; there were also schemes for two clients in Birkenhead, fitting out rooms in existing houses beginning in 1902. It is notable that the two most lavish of these, Queensborough Terrace and Garden Corner, were adaptations to existing houses. The individual pieces made for Queensborough Terrace have, in most important cases, been mentioned individually in earlier chapters and no more will be said of this interior. Garden Corner, which was in many ways a similar project though several years later, will be looked at in some detail.

The typical Voysey room is notable, first of all, for its lowness, emphasized by low door architrave height – anyone of or slightly over six feet in height will collect a few bruises before he learns – and a low picture rail, lower than door

58a
Contemporary photograph showing the study at The Orchard, Voysey's own house at Chorleywood, c.1900.

58b
Contemporary photograph showing the hall
at The Orchard, c.1900.

58c
Contemporary photograph showing the
dining-room at The Orchard, c.1900.

height. Doors are cottage-like, planked not panelled; chimney-pieces usually, in
the main rooms, tiled. Ceilings are plain, white, without cornice mouldings of any
sort. The walls below the picture rail – which is plain, not moulded – might for
preference be panelled with plain, vertical boarding, either white oak as the
furniture or, more economically, deal painted white. Failing that, a plain, painted
surface or, very occasionally, a patterned paper. Floors might be a plain, natural
finish – oak boarding, again, or quarry tile or slate – with, in the more comfortable
family rooms, perhaps a patterned carpet. These points are borne out well in three
contemporary photographs showing the study, hall and dining-room of The
Orchard at Chorleywood arranged as it was shortly after it was built (58a,b,c).
Into this very unfussy interior were introduced, surprisingly, quite a lot of small
objects – ceramics, lamps, pictures, clocks and general knick-knacks (including de
rigueur a vase of honesty and a peacock feather or two) giving to the whole a well
lived-in appearance. An exactly similar impression is given by one of the
Birkenhead rooms (59) a couple of years later than The Orchard; materials here
are plain, though of the best quality, and there is similar evidence of a good
sprinkling of small 'art-objects' about the place. Here oak panelling is used – the
budget at The Orchard perhaps did not permit of this expensive finish – and the
chimney-piece is tiled in large squares, probably of the rich green-blues that
Voysey favoured. The brass fender is to Voysey's design as is, almost certainly, the
light fitting; on the wall can be seen a circular gilded mirror with low-relief
carving. The photograph is presumed to show the dining-room of 1902 for Mrs
van Gruisen, at Bidston Road, Birkenhead though Voysey did in the same year
work at another house for a Miss McKay, also in Birkenhead.

From 1905 to 1907 Voysey worked on two buildings where he handled both
construction and fitting out. These were Hollymount, at Knotty Green near
Beaconsfield for C.T.Burke; and The Homestead at Frinton-on-Sea for
S.C.Turner. The drawing-room at Hollymount (60) shows the small, circular

59
Contemporary photograph showing the
dining-room of a house at Birkenhead, *c.*1903.

60
Contemporary photograph showing the
drawing-room of Hollymount for C.T.Burke
at Knotty Green, *c.*1907.

61
Contemporary photograph showing the
drawing-cum-billiard-room at The
Homestead, Frinton-on-Sea, for S.C. Turner,
*c.*1907.

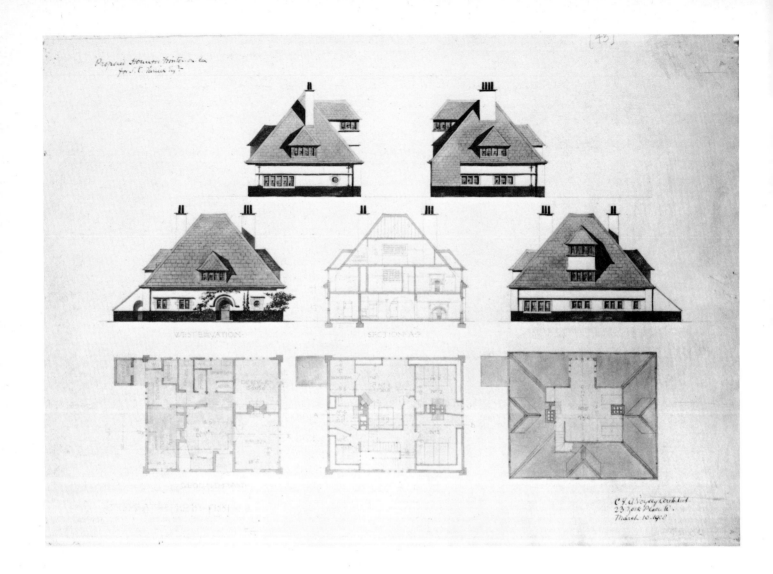

62
Design for a house at Frinton-on-Sea, Essex,
for S.C.Turner, 1908; elevations, cross sections
and plans. Unexecuted.

window opening which Voysey favoured and used in many houses to cast a little
extra light into the fireplace area without depriving it of the sense of enclosed
comfort. The liking for a very high mantelpiece shows clearly, and the clutter of
small objects. The lamp, fire-irons and fender are all to Voysey's design. The
circular table mentioned above is clearly seen and two versions of the single-heart
chair; also a plain carpet with patterned frieze, again Voysey's work. The piano
also is interesting; Voysey designed, early in the 1890s, two piano cases, one of
them complex and ornate; towards the end of that decade he also designed a
slightly plainer case for production by Messrs Collard and Collard. The case
shown here appears very similar to that design.

The Homestead was built for S.C.Turner, an important client and a bachelor who was prepared to give Voysey a free hand both to build and to furnish his sea-side home. The house is L-shaped and medium-sized, the feature of the ground floor being a large billiard-cum-sitting room, clearly an all-purpose relaxation and entertainment room (61). The heavily beamed ceiling is notable, as is the almost excessive austerity of the white tiled ingle-nook with its flat arch top, the plain whitewashed walls with exposed beams over, the quarry tile floor only partially carpeted. The set of fire-irons unfortunately almost mask the panel of four tiles with bird and flower motifs which are a token contribution to breaking the austerity of the tiled surface. The chairs are interesting; two of the standard easy chairs as noted above and an unusual variation on the lathe-back chair. The billiard-table is also by Voysey, a design from circa 1899 originally drawn for the Revd Grane for Norney and later sold to Thurston and Co., the billiard-table makers, who offered it as part of their regular range. In the background can be seen a Chesterfield, also mentioned above. The external appearance of this house is shown in 44. Strangely – by way of digression – Voysey made drawings from Nov. 1907 to mid-1908, when The Homestead was already built, for another smaller house for Turner at Frinton; one of these schemes is shown (62), dated March 1908, and it is a pity that one of the intriguing small designs was not executed. Why Turner should have planned another house in this way is not known, unless he felt that The Homestead was too big for him alone.

The second really substantial commission for fitting out an interior, some years later than 23 Queensborough Terrace, was the house on the embankment at Chelsea, belonging to E.J.Horniman for whom Voysey had built Lowicks at Frensham; for this project, known as Garden Corner (designed 1906–7), Voysey had a very free hand and, apparently, a large budget. He began by mercilessly lowering the ceiling heights where he thought it necessary, as is clearly shown in (63a). With this preliminary carried out he added excellent fixtures such as the staircase (63b) and bedroom furniture (63c). The library (63d) featured a beamed ceiling and the glass-fronted cupboards with elaborate glazing pattern as fitted some years before at New Place at Haslemere. Into this carefully prepared interior was added a wide range of furniture, perhaps the key piece being a four-poster bed (63e) which unfortunately does not survive, so far as is known. Capping each post is the figure of a bird, presumably in cast bronze and looking like the standard fitting which Elsley and Co. produced for Voysey, which is a realization of Voysey's mystic comment:

> You shall perch four eagles on my bedposts to drive away bad spirits, as
> the Byzantines believed, and rest my fire irons on the backs of brass
> cats, not dogs, for cats are the most faithful fireside dwellers.[7]

In fact this interior seems in many ways to be a working out in practice of the precepts which Voysey put forward in his lecture, now several times quoted, delivered to the Carpenters' Company in 1909 and subsequently published. It seems therefore fitting to look at the illustrations of Garden Corner to the accompaniment of Voysey's own words:

> You will arrange my rooms with their furniture so that each piece has
> the place most suited for its use, with light helping to make it more

63a
Contemporary photograph of Garden Corner, Chelsea Embankment, London, for E.J.Horniman, 1906–7, a complete installation of an interior by Voysey into an existing house. The drawing room, c.1908.

63b
Contemporary photograph showing the head of the staircase at Garden Corner, c.1908.

63c
Contemporary photograph showing fitted furniture and chimney-piece in one of the bedrooms at Garden Corner, c.1908.

63d
Contemporary photograph showing the library at Garden Corner, c.1908.

126

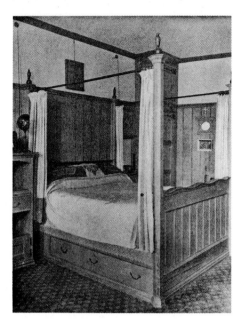

63e
Contemporary photograph showing the four-poster bed installed in the master bedroom at Garden Corner, *c*.1908.

useful, so that we feel no single bit of furniture is quarelling with or harassing another, and everything shall have its useful purpose. Thus proportion and grace and the intention to serve a useful purpose will provide the very best elements of beauty, and ornaments will be little required. If you give me one or two in each room, such as pictures and sculpture, they will be infinitely more impressive alone than when in a crowd. You cannot listen to two people talking at the same time, so we don't want a thousand ornaments to be bawling at us all day long.[8]

From door furniture to four-poster beds, picture-rail moulding to tiled chimney-pieces, Voysey liked to have every detail of his houses and their contents under his control where possible. His approach was not conventional; often this is given away by his throwaway lines which also, incidentally, give us the clue to his keen sense of humour. From start to finish Voysey sees himself, the architect, providing a setting in which a life-style can be lived out to the fullest and in which a strict ideal is suggested and, sometimes, imposed:

I want no finger plates, because they suggest that I keep dirty fingers in my house.[9]

His rule as architect over client would be, if he could manage it, a despotism, albeit a benevolent one. The key to understanding the surroundings which Voysey aimed to produce for his clients is to see that he did feel a religious fervour about his work; he did feel it to be proper to evangelize, architecturally speaking, in order to convert the client to his point of view. He did respect the right of the client to have strong feelings – the correspondence quoted in chapter 4 with Cecil Fitch demonstrates this clearly – but the client had to fight to have this right recognized. Like most missionaries, Voysey would bully if he could, would give in on certain points if forced to in order to gain the main ground, and if he saw too many of his cherished ideals slipping away in the fight with the client, would throw up the commission, however good, to preserve his integrity.

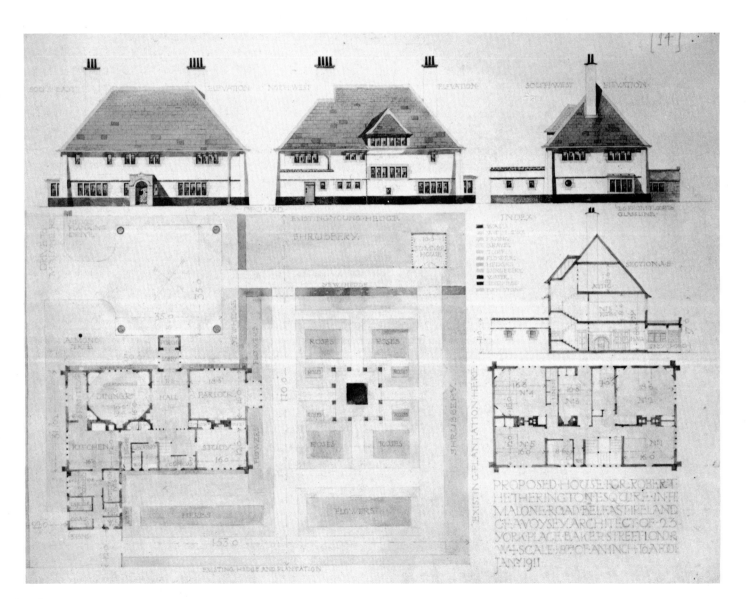

Chapter 6   **The Practice in Decline, 1910–41**

There were no major executed buildings in the last thirty years of Voysey's life and career; there were, indeed, none that would merit being called substantial. The reason is not that Voysey was unwilling to work, but that the clients stopped coming to him. Since other instances have shown that a well-known architect can be difficult, idiosyncratic and expensive yet still attract more clients than he knows how to cope with, the only conclusion left is that the clients ceased to produce commissions because the Voysey house was not what they wanted. In addition, the implication must be that Voysey was not prepared or able to mould his work into a form that was acceptable to the client. These last thirty years, then, were not busy ones; work trickled in, small commissions often from clients who had used Voysey previously and whose motive in returning to him may have been satisfaction, sentiment or even, one suspects, occasionally charity. Yet there is a considerable interest in these years for the student of Voysey's work, stemming largely from the various unexecuted projects with which Voysey occupied himself. Some were commissions or possible commissions which, for reasons now unknown, failed to be realized; others were competition entries which did not win; mostly even this kind of activity was over by the middle of the 1920s but Voysey was by this time an elderly man, reaching his seventies.

The last executed house of any distinction and size was designed in 1911 for Robert Hetherington to be built in the Malone Road at Belfast (64). It was a simple rectangular house with a hipped roof broken by a single hipped dormer on the garden front. There is also in the design a small stone porch – the appearance and means of construction of the house are otherwise conventional Voysey – though this was omitted in the house as built. In plan the main rooms open off a central hall with a rear staircase, the dining-room being formed to an octagonal shape. The plan includes details of the garden layout and a small summer house.

In 1914 came two designs for houses which – though not built – were substantial in size and indicated not only the continuation of Voysey's interest in the use of an adapted Gothic motif in his work but also a new complexity of form and layout, based on the use of those finishes and materials which we accept as part of his established working pattern. Slightly the earlier of the two schemes – the drawings dated around June 1914 – was a house for H.Tingey. There were several schemes for this house which was to be near Thatcham and Cold Ash in Berkshire; the first, which is illustrated (65), is based on a courtyard layout, the others adopting a T-shape. Roughcast is shown to be used, with a slate roof and stone dressing to the

64
Design for a house in Malone Road, Belfast, N.Ireland, for R.Hetherington, 1911; elevations, section and plans. Executed substantially as shown here with the porch omitted.

65
Design for a house near Thatcham and Cold Ash, Berkshire, for H. Tingey, 1914; elevations and block plan. Unexecuted.

leaded windows. Several features, though, differentiate this design from the houses we are accustomed to see. First is the complexity of layout, indicated best here by the use of the courtyard form and by a variety of roof surfaces and heights which the illustration clearly shows. Eaves and roof lines vary in height and also appear at both first- and second-storey height. Fenestration is irregular, as seen most clearly on the north elevation. Then there is the use of detailing: pointed arch openings of different forms to all the external doors; a square quasi-medieval tower which, ironically, was intended to house thoroughly modern wireless equipment; crenellations to this tower and to the single-storey glazed walkway which closes the fourth side of the courtyard with its continuous strip of fenestration; the figure of a winged archer shown on this single-storey stretch of roof. This was clearly a house which was seriously discussed with the client, for it evolved through four schemes and it is a great disappointment that, for whatever reasons, the discussions clearly broke down and it was never built.

Similar to this proposed house was one which was designed a little later, around October 1914, to be built at Ashmansworth in Berkshire for a client with the delightful name of Arthur aBeckett Terrell. There are many links between this design (66) and that mentioned above. The same courtyard plan form; an intricacy of roof forms which, for Voysey, was quite startling; a square tower and a glazed walkway, both crenellated; the use of the pointed arch to form openings; a figure, the precise form of which is difficult to make out, which is in this case mounted above the main entrance. The main rooms and bedrooms are grouped in the L-shaped two-storey portion of the house, running along the north-west and south-west sides of the square. There are in addition single-storey projecting rooms flanking the main entrance, one housing a 'motor shed', the other a morning-

66
Design for a house at Ashmansworth, near Newbury, Berkshire, for Arthur a Beckett Terrell, 1914; elevations, sections and plans. Unexecuted.

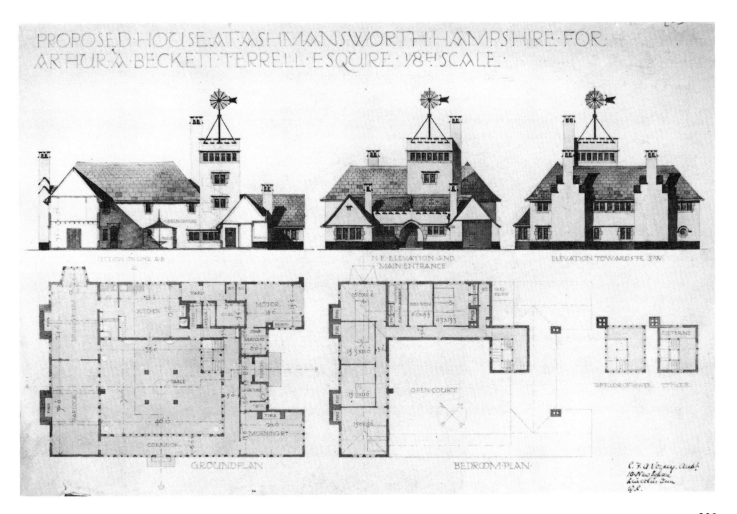

67
Design for a house at Laughton, near Market
Harborough, Leicestershire, for W. Taylor,
*c.*1920; line drawing of south (entrance)
elevation and first-floor plan. Unexecuted.

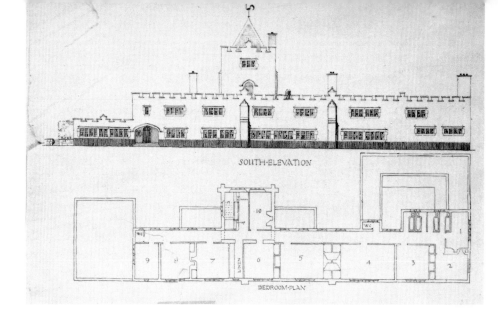

68a and b
Design for a house at Jihlava, Czechoslovakia,
for Karl Löwe, 1922; line drawings of front
and rear elevations. Unexecuted so far as is
known.

room. The glazed corridor then links this room with the rest of the main rooms. A windmill perched on top of the tower adds a final air of incongruity to this design.

In their move towards a domestic form of greater complexity and with a freer use of decorative detail – we might infer that a greater luxury of material and finish were also implied – these two designs point to a wish to move into a more ambitious type of domestic architecture. That the desire for bigger commissions may have been stimulated largely by the failure of any commissions at all to appear is a possibility. However the more reasoned and reasonable view is that Voysey did wish to produce a new style of rather more lavish buildings at this stage in his life. The same impression is gained from two unexecuted designs of a few years later, just after the Great War, again the two designs appearing close together and with obvious links between them. The earlier and smaller dates from 1920, though Voysey's own *Black Book* notes, erroneously, that the design is of 1929. The house was designed for a client named William Taylor to be built at Laughton, near Market Harborough (67); the facing materials are conventional, roughcast with stone dressings. The layout is a long, rectangular two-storey block; here, though, resemblances to the typical Voysey house cease. This design is for a house with a flat roof and a prominent tower on the north front, housing main entrance and staircase. The detailing is more overtly and consistently Gothic in form than anything Voysey had previously produced; crenellations run all round and the wall buttresses are capped with ogee-shaped mouldings. Symmetrically placed on the centre line of the south elevation – the tower is off-centre on the north – is a single, large grotesque figure, crouched between two crenellations. A steep pitch roof rises from the top of the tower, capped by a weather-cock, though a second scheme retains a flat roof instead. There are various other differences in the second scheme but it is essentially similar. This house designed for Taylor is again, like the two designs of 1914, a substantial and elaborate venture displaying a continuing fascination with the use of adapted Gothic forms; while the designs of 1914 appeared to be Voysey houses tempered by the addition of Gothic detailing, this 1920 project is more outspoken and would, in the climate of post-war domestic architecture, have been a decided oddity if built. Two years later, in 1922, another chance to design a very substantial house came Voysey's way. This time it was from the very unlikely source of a Czech client, Karl Löwe, who wanted a house to be designed for building in his native country. It is unlikely, though not absolutely impossible, that the building was erected; certainly Voysey did not himself supervise the building, and no house stands so far as is known in this original form. There were two schemes for the house, the earlier of which is shown (68a and b). Both schemes were for a house E-shaped in plan with a central projecting porch and side wings closed by an iron fence running the width of the front. In elevation the first scheme employs roughcast with stone dressings; the steep pitched roofs run down to eaves at ground-floor window level, against which the substantial crenellated porch contrasts by rising sheer to three-storey height, the full height of the main house. The front elevation has four dormer windows, hipped, two at first- and two at second-floor level. On the rear elevation the two bay windows are square with crenellations over and the first floor (there is on this elevation no second) is lit by a row of five hipped dormers, three large and two small. Ranges of outbuildings left and right are all single-storey and emphasized by steep pitched hipped roofs. Two factors are evident; first is the visual complexity of the scheme, by contrast with any of Voysey's earlier work; second is the heavy emphasis on symmetry, broken only by the main chimney-stacks. This again is not an element that one expects to see in Voysey's work. Both of these features are carried through into the second, revised scheme for this house; indeed here the effect is one of even greater formalization which contrasts oddly with the vernacular, rural style of the work. This scheme has a centre bay with a gable flanked by castellated bays with a belfry and lantern over. On the front are six small dormers at first-floor level, two larger and hipped at second floor; on the rear are now shown nine dormers at first-floor level, five large and four small, alternating. Both schemes are impressive and it is this project, backed by the earlier for the Laughton house, that makes one wish that Voysey had continued to build in the later part of his career. The move from the austerity of the styling of his earlier houses to the Gothic indiscipline of those few buildings around 1910 appears now to be resolved and a rustic vernacular lives comfortably side by side with the Gothic stylistic motifs. The sense of plain form is as strong as ever but less restrained so a greater freedom and complexity emerge. In plan also, although these late schemes do not achieve a great subtlety, they demonstrate a clear willingness to change and to try something new. It is a sad irony that at the very time when he could have produced something substantially different from the work of his early years, his considerable reputation seems to have temporarily sunk so far that no client came forward. Also it is sad that it may well have been that very post-war austerity and shortage of cash that, while it encouraged the development of a major new domestic vernacular revival based on those small rural houses that Voysey had excelled at building, excluded him from making his move to more substantial projects.

Public building was never a field into which Voysey made any inroads; there had been a few projects earlier but nothing was built. In 1901 there was a design for a Grammar School at Lincoln, in 1904 an unsuccessful competition entry for a Museum and Library at Limerick. Both had strong affinities with the Sandersons factory described in chapter 4. In 1914 came another competition entry, again unsuccessful, for Supreme Courts in the City of Ottawa, a competition arranged by the Canadian Government. Voysey's scheme was frankly Gothic, as one might have expected from this period of his life. The detailing is Perpendicular and quite restrained, except on the dominant central gateway and tower with its profusion of crockets. These schemes all lead up to what was the most substantial and the most curious of the designs for public buildings which, if built, would have had a radical impact on central London. In 1923, following the demolition of the old Devonshire House in Piccadilly, facing where Green Park Tube station now stands, there was a competition for the design of its successor. Voysey suggested in a letter to the *Builder*, accompanied by a sketch design (69), that three identical tower blocks should be built for residential use. In form the blocks as sketched suggest nothing so much as the hand-painted clock case of 1895 described earlier; four massive corner towers – housing emergency staircases – support a carcase of

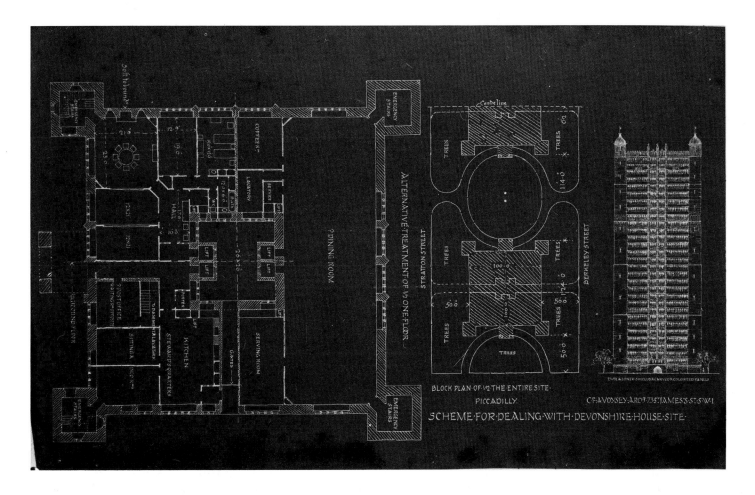

69
Design for the Devonshire House site,
Piccadilly, London, a competition entry, 1923;
specimen plans and elevation. Unexecuted.

thirty floors grouped round a central lift and light well and offering a range of living accommodation and services, including large communal dining-rooms and shops. It is a curious blend of two ideas: Baillie Scott had been putting forward some twenty years earlier[2] a scheme for what he called 'Co-operative houses', with a justification which rings strangely to modern ears used to the ramifications of the high-rise controversy:

> Anyone who has penetrated to the less fashionable outskirts of a
> modern town must have observed those long rows of mean dwellings
> which encroach on the surrounding country, and must have felt what a
> melancholy thing it must be to live there. One cannot but think that
> there should be some better way of living than that which finds
> expression in these sordid streets ... In this matter the savage who decks
> his primitive dwelling with brightly painted carving is more advanced
> than we, and of all the habitations of man, surely none have quite
> reached such an expression of sordid meanness as the modern street of
> suburban villa residences.[3]

135

70

Clock designed by Voysey for himself or a
member of his family, *c*.1910–12.

Baillie Scott goes on to suggest that functions such as cooking and heating should
be communal though he points out the basic problem of the conflicting claims of
privacy and comfort competing with those of convenience and economy:

> ... for while, as the copy-book maxim says, 'union is strength', the
> strength of the community is generally obtainable only at some
> sacrifice of its individuals, and while the bundle of arrows is not so
> readily broken as the single shaft, their feathers may be sorely ruffled by
> their close contact with each other.[4]

Voysey goes a little further than this in the Devonshire House scheme in that not
only the means of comfort and ease – communal eating and heating – are involved
but also provision of other services and on a much larger scale than Baillie Scott
was suggesting. What is strange is that Voysey is also echoing the type of thinking
which was to lead, at its height, to the Unités d'Habitation of Le Corbusier,
typified by that at Marseilles begun in 1947. This puts a simplistic gloss on the
complex issue of the developments of the past eighty years in mass housing; it is
made to clarify not that vexed issue but the simpler one of Voysey's own thought
processes. One suspects that Voysey's ideal lay a good deal closer to the Baillie
Scott of 1906 than the Le Corbusier of 1947, that his aim was not so much the
'vertical city' as the 'vertical feudal village' though it is not clear in this case quite
who the Squire was to be. The loosely medievalized cladding of his proposed
structure certainly bears out this interpretation. Nevertheless the Devonshire
House proposal is an intriguing part of Voysey's thinking at this time and not to be
dismissed too lightly. It is ironical that the man who, more than any other single
designer, produced in the 1890s the model on which the ribbon development mass
housing of the 1920s was to base its units was, while that very mass housing boom
went on, giving a kind of tacit support in his Devonshire House scheme to the
ideas propounded by a new generation – and a very different one – of architectural
activists. We often hear of an implicit link between Voysey and the founders of the
Modern Movement so it is pleasing to be able to see at least the outlines of an actual
or explicit one.

These were the major architectural projects of the latter part of Voysey's life.
From the Devonshire House scheme in 1923 until his death in 1941 there was
practically nothing built of importance and only the occasional scheme which
attracts notice, such as another unsuccessful competition design for a large
Exhibition Hall in Manchester in 1933. In 1931 a retrospective exhibition of his
work was held at the Batsford Gallery, indicating that his reputation was still
alive; the occasion was sufficiently important for Sir Edwin Lutyens to contribute
the catalogue foreword. The formal honours which one would expect to accrue to
a man of Voysey's reputation did accrue through this long period, but slowly. In
1924 the Mastership of the Art Workers' Guild; in 1936 he was made Designer for
Industry by the Royal Society of Arts; only in 1940, the year before his death, was
he awarded the Royal Gold Medal of the Royal Institute of British Architects.

71
Toilet glass, pre-1919.

Furniture designs, 1910–41

Voysey's production of furniture designs after 1910 mirrors the progress of his architectural work; first the output changes noticeably in type, then it drops sharply off to almost nothing. An oak clock case of c.1910–12 (70) has all the plainness of what we regard as traditional Voysey furniture; the untreated oak surfaces are relieved only by simple mouldings and metal fittings, in this case absolutely plain spherical bronze feet. The face has a standard Voysey numbering, yet the hands are remarkably intricate in their design. The form of the clock also, though compact and uncluttered, has the juxtaposition of square base with octagonal face; the noticeable change in this design is that, unlike all of the furniture large and small previously produced, its form is not architectural. The emphasis on structure – as for instance in the way that the supports, corner posts or legs, of his furniture are always stressed in the construction – has gone and this clock simply stands in a form calculated to house its working parts and make its face clearly visible. The toilet glass of 1919 or a little earlier (71) shows an increase in the use of moulding and contour; the form of this piece, with its freer curves

72
Contemporary photograph of a sideboard or carving table; it is thought that at least two examples were made, the first in 1912, the second c.1923, and one example survives.

and the use of a profile bird's head as a handle for the wooden ratchet which fixes the angle of tilt, recalls Voysey's first furniture design, the Swan chair. This is not so surprising when we remember that the Swan chair was based, more freely than was customary with Voysey, on medieval and post-medieval precedent. If these two pieces suggest, in an oblique way, a move away from the austere discipline we expect of Voysey and towards a concern with the use of medieval motifs, how much more so does the carving table (72) which seems to have been designed originally in 1912 and re-used much later in 1923. The dominant feature is the group of four carved angels – the carving is by William Aumonier – which are singing grace grouped around the surface of the table. It was not unknown for Voysey to suggest the use of carved figures as cappings for supports on his furniture; a plain round or square cap was the usual, with sometimes a mushroom finial being suggested in drawings. This use, however, of overtly medievalized carved figures harks back to another early piece, the hanging cupboard which dates from pre-1896 (see 26) and has two medievalized carved figures as cappings. Certainly the carving table has the air about it of a piece of furniture intended for use at least in a vicarage or vestry if not in a church itself.

A good many years after these designs Voysey produced his last, and the contrast is interesting. In the intervening years there had been, according to the *Black Book*, a good deal of furniture of which we retain no record at all. Much of it, we can assume, was made up from existing earlier designs, perhaps slightly modified to suit. There are enough instances of this recorded for us to know that it happened frequently; there is, though, the possibility that other new designs may exist, unknown to us. What is certain is that, probably in 1934 which is the date the *Black Book* gives us (it is not reliable) a suite of furniture was produced for Voysey's niece Ella and her new husband, Robert Donat. There was also a scheme, in 1936, to build a house for the couple in Hampstead but this was abandoned. Part of that suite is shown (73) and it is clear that the Gothic motif is now firmly allied to Voysey's established style of furniture design. The piece is, as ever, impeccably made and the use of turned stretchers on the stool should also be noted; wood turning was not a feature which ever appeared in earlier work.

Even disregarding the decade before his death when Voysey might quite decently and deservedly have been in retirement it is clear that his energetic career had a very long tail and that this was probably not of his choosing. In view of the suggestions we have that in those years he was capable of producing interesting work and work which showed a clear development from what went before, this is cause for great regret. It does seem that he was the victim partly of history – the day of the country house and substantial private patronage was over – and partly of a personality which, in professional though not by all accounts in private terms, was too unyielding. It is an unresolvable dilemma for had he been more flexible and compromising by nature he would never have been able to contribute as extensively as he did and may well have remained simply part of the second-rate group of late Victorian and Edwardian architects. Nevertheless one's feeling is that these long years of enforced inactivity were not particularly happy ones for Voysey.

73
Dressing table and stool for Mr and Mrs
Robert Donat, 1934.

Chapter 7   **The Voysey Inheritance**

Individuality

Voysey has been a considerable influence on the younger generation. It may
be due to him that rough plaster has become the fashionable finish for
exterior walls, perhaps too it was his influence that has produced so many
advocates of the low ceiling, of which he was so fond. Some of Voysey's
external features, such as corner buttresses, have also been imitated.
At all events Voysey is the most individualistic of the busy domestic
architects in London today, and his courage in seeking new ways and
displaying his own personal art to good advantage is as rare as it is
refreshing in the prevailing conservatism of the London movement.[1]

This contemporary assessment from Muthesius has an air of objectivity – what
native critic would have dared to refer to the 'prevailing conservatism' of
architectural trends over the years when Voysey was forming his career? Yet it is
true that, however inspired and avant-garde it may have been, the work of such
men as Voysey, Baillie Scott, Newton, even Rennie Mackintosh was in various
crucial ways 'conservative'. It is only in understanding this apparent conflict in a
creative style, between the forces of conservatism or tradition and those of
individuality or innovation, that it is possible to understand the domestic
architecture of the years surrounding the birth of the present century, and the role
that Voysey played in forming it and what came after it.

During the Great War that effectively undermined and eventually destroyed
the world he knew and many of the principles and standards that were dear to
him, Voysey produced the best sustained account of his views in a book entitled
Individuality.[2] His insight, often erratic in matters not related to the particular skills
he possessed, was on this occasion particularly keen:

Surely it is evident that the most far-reaching and important effect of
the present war, will be to force men to distinguish more clearly
between intellectual and spiritual culture, and thus to encourage the
latter and by so doing strengthen and sustain individuality.[3]

Had he only said 'the former' instead of 'the latter' he would have been right; even
so it is an intriguing remark. It points the way from the individuality of his own
career first to the mock individuality of the acres of small suburban villas which
were the speculative builders' acknowledgment of Voysey's particular genius;
second to the substantial individuality, which he abhorred, of the Modern

Movement which, like it or not, kept architecture and design moving in the interregnum between the two great world wars.

Much of *Individuality* was based upon Voysey's perception of the way in which his work and views related to the English architectural tradition. Muthesius, for instance, in *Das englische Haus*, claims that Voysey cast tradition aside in his work (remember that Muthesius was writing before those developments we have seen where Voysey later in his career turned more and more to medieval inspiration) yet Voysey himself was always much exercised by the way in which his work related to English tradition – the two are not contradictory. It is important to understand this for its effect on Voysey's work was substantial:

> Men cannot be honest while imitating the sentiments of others which
> they often neither feel or understand.[4]

Voysey was at once fiercely parochial, for he believed that one could 'feel or understand' only those sentiments which arose from one's own culture and country, and also whole-heartedly opposed to materialism:

> The lack of noble sentiment in our modern buildings is due to the
> materialism of the age, which has led to the assumption of a foreign
> style, and the acquisition of material qualities only. Thought and
> feeling are ignored, hence the works are still-born.[5]

This led him naturally to the vernacular tradition of his own country for it was only here that he could find roots which he could regard as truly his own, which were untainted by the stylistic excesses which he attributed both to foreign-ness and to excessive wealth, both being for him corrupting influences. This puritanical severity is still further emphasized by the constraints he then felt in the ways in which he could make use of the limited heritage he recognized:

> Reverence for the past is admirable when exercised by the individual
> for his own guidance, but mischievous when imposed upon others.[6]

It only remained then for Voysey to define the way in which the designer, influenced by tradition in this special way, could bring his influence to bear on the lives of people. First his field of reference should be large and he should not be too proud to deal with any small detail:

> ... it must follow that matter in any way affected by man must partake
> of and reflect his spirit, his thoughts and feelings. We recognize this in
> the Cathedral – why, then, not in the lamp-post?[7]

Second he should not let himself be influenced by whim or fashion:

> If we could set our hearts on proclaiming nothing but the truth about
> ourselves, the fear of public opinion would vanish, standards of fashion
> would cease to exist, and our homes would then be furnished only with
> what we needed for daily use; and each object would have to be as
> beautiful as we could make it or procure it, in order to harmonise with
> our feeling, rather than with an assumed convention.[8]

In this way Voysey defined the limits of the individuality he felt; it was an idiosyncratic view but one which led, logically and inexorably enough, from the love and knowledge of the English vernacular bred into him from his Yorkshire childhood, through the puritanical strain inculcated in him, again at an early age, to the wish to surround himself and all men with carefully conceived, designed and wrought objects.

Reinforcing the sense of individuality which Voysey felt and in which he worked was the constant background and accompaniment of his distinctive religious and moralistic views. There was a general basis for this which was rooted in the earlier part of the nineteenth century; as has been said above, Voysey was greatly impressed and moulded by the views of A.W.N.Pugin. Pugin had combined, to a degree unique in the history of British architecture and design since the Middle Ages ended, a sense of religion and practicality; his work and his God were tightly bound together. In a less demonstrative way, befitting one who was as close to Puritanism as was Pugin to the highest reaches of Catholicism (several of Voysey's early clients were Quakers), Voysey shared this preoccupation. So on various occasions we find him referring to the high moralists of art, either of his own day or of an earlier one. He speaks warmly of March Phillipps; and when he seeks a source for the basis of his own philosophy it is to one of the formative British moralists of his century that he refers:

As Carlyle has said, the spiritual is the parent and first cause of the practical.[9]

What is convincing above all about Voysey's sense of religion in art is that he so consistently adhered to it throughout his long career. And he was aware of the dangers which it contained:

Although reading the newspapers as little as possible, I am yet impressed by the frequency with which we meet the statement that, 'an artist must express himself' . . . The writers who mean by it to emphasise the importance of absolute sincerity are of course right; but to the young mind it may mean egoism, which is the most poisonous perversion of individuality. The very wish to express oneself is corrupting to the soul and intoxicating to personal vanity.[10]

Gothic and Grotesque

It is important to remember two recurring themes in Voysey's work. His reputation rests on the principles of plainness and simplicity. Walls are white roughcast on the outside, untreated oak panelling or plaster surface devoid of decorative mouldings inside; dimensions are modest; everything is understated. Two things disturb this consistency and it is necessary to realize why they do so; the first is the grotesque form; the second the Gothic. The grotesque has been pointed to several times in the preceding chapters and recurs throughout Voysey's career: the porch at St Dunstan's Road, the sundial at Norney, the corbelled carved heads at Broadleys, the profile incised in the bedroom chair and so on. Other instances have not been specifically mentioned, the most notable being the small devil which Voysey worked up himself for casting in bronze or plaster and which was a caricature of himself – this particular grotesque was also carved in much larger form, in stone, for the house he built for Müntzer at Guildford. The same theme, the use of the grotesque form or figure, also recurs often among the flowers and birds of his pattern design output. His use of it is very medieval; it is part jest, for very often we know or suspect that his forms are based on those of the particular client; part serious for it brings a cautionary personal note into the buildings where it appears, a reminder of ephemerality, human vanity or whatever. What is fascinating is that the note that the grotesque strikes in Voysey's work is so discordant when seen against the pattern and background of what we expect from him. Yet it brings a vital element of warmth to his work and emphasizes his basic humanity. Similar in some of its roots is the prepossession with Gothic form; but where the grotesque relates to Voysey's own sense of humanity, this relates rather to his sense of propriety. He speaks of:

> ... the Gothic principles of evolving our homes out of local conditions
> and requirements.[11]

He goes on in the same piece to attack the principles of Classical symmetry and adds:

> The Gothic process is the exact opposite; outside appearances are
> evolved from internal fundamental conditions; staircases and windows
> come where most convenient to use ... the creation of a beautiful
> Gothic building, instead of being a conception based on a temple made
> with hands, is based on the temple of a human soul.[12]

In this sense it can be seen that a 'Gothic' principle did infuse all of his work; this, though, is a highly specialized and limited interpretation of the Gothic and in surveying his work in the previous chapters what has emerged is that Gothic forms were particularly apparent in it both early in his career and late, but hardly at all in between. Certainly Voysey himself was always aware of the conflict of interest here and this may account for his abandonment of any Gothic element in the best and most productive part of his life. For on the one hand he was emphatic:

> The revivalism of the present century ... has done more to stamp out
> men's artistic common sense and understanding than any movement I
> know. The unintelligent, unappreciative use of the works of the past,
> which is the rule, has surrounded us at every turn with deadly
> dulness.[13]

And later in his life:

> Surely a national style would be both possible and desirable as it was in
> the Tudor period, if allowed to develop out of national conditions and
> requirements. It is the ingrafting of a foreign style, or manner of
> buildings, which is so poisonous and utterly subversive of any national
> growth.[14]

So for many years he was scrupulous about keeping any actual element of the Gothic out of his work though he believed – and with justification – that it was imbued with the same spirit which had moved the Gothic builders. Again, there are echoes of Pugin. As he grew older and as his practice began to shrink his feeling seemed to strengthen that he should acknowledge the link that bound him to the style and traditions of medieval Britain and to the early part of the Victorian Gothic Revival personified for him by Pugin.

The Inheritance

This book began from the precept that Voysey was a key figure and has attempted, in monograph form, to outline the progression of his work through his career, the principal developments it showed, the major buildings and designs, the unfulfilled possibilities. All of this has been done without a great deal of reference to the other events of the years covered and to the influence that Voysey's work might have had on others. This course has been chosen without real apology, for these facets are the subject not of another chapter but of another book. Voysey worked on his own; he did not, generally speaking, school pupils; he did not court publicity; when he spoke publicly it was not to any smart set or to potential clients but by means of lectures delivered principally to fellow architects and designers and craftsmen – and this he did only infrequently. His writings, interesting to the student, were not compulsive, the overlay of moralizing being quite a heavy price to pay for the valuable hints gained. He did not show the facility in print, the fluency and sense of flair and inventiveness which Baillie Scott achieved; he did not, like Lethaby, become a mentor and instructor who spoke to everybody and particularly to generations of students; he did not reach the potential clients, mix in society and sell his genius in the flamboyant style of Lutyens; nor did he parade his talent across Europe as did Mackintosh. In a way he was an architect's architect; his stand of principle, his dedication, his purism throughout his career, were probably more understandable to those who shared his aim to design beautiful, simple, workable things than to those who needed to commission a modern house. Only they could fully comprehend the dedication and the unwillingness to offer compromise which his best work showed.

Yet for all this Voysey enjoyed a considerable success and reputation in his lifetime and has, more or less consistently since his death, retained a substantial aura, a sense in the even moderately well-informed onlooker that he stood somewhere near to the centre of the architectural events of his day. He is a lesson in what constitutes the basis of reputation and nowhere is this more true than in the impact he made in Europe and particularly in Germany. He was no traveller and so any knowledge of him and his work outside England was transmitted by written word and word of mouth. From an early date his work figured in the German periodical, *Dekorative Kunst*; it also appeared at the 1900 Paris Exhibition; and of course, as has been mentioned, he was praised in Hermann Muthesius's book, *Das englische Haus* which, appearing in the first decade of this century, gave wide currency to the events of English architecture of the period.

Nearer home one has to think of Voysey in terms of the massive housebuilding, the suburban development, of the early part of this century. This is not a subject susceptible of facile interpretation or of quick summary; too many forces are involved, social, political and economic, before the basic but not pre-emptive issue of design can be introduced. What Voysey and a handful of colleagues offered was a style of domestic vernacular which appealed to a wide public; it had a sense of tradition, discernible bits of half-timbering and leaded windows as well as more subtle devices. It was pleasingly assymetrical and rambling, qualities inexorably suggestive of a kind of freedom and improvisation appreciated by many people. It was also, in terms of superficial impact on the eye, refreshingly new and could not be mistaken for any other of the prevalent domestic styles of the previous century. So among the many styles that remained popular, both in the rather dignified medium-sized country-house building in the years just before the Great War and in the lower and middle-class speculative housing boom of the 1920s and later, the style that became known as stockbroker Tudor or mock-Tudor has always more than held its own. Indeed it has come to signify a whole aspect of the British class system and British life. It should be stressed that in this general sense those nicknames cover both the detached suburban house type and the more mass-produced ribbon development house. It would indeed require another book to define the various influences at work here and to allocate specific roles to Voysey and to Newton, Harrison Townsend, Arnold Mitchell and others from his immediate contemporaries in the forming of such movements; one would also need to look back carefully to the sources which influenced them, the generation of Norman Shaw. The conclusion here can be no more than that Voysey played an important role in these movements. He designed houses that intrigued people, caused them to think and led them to incorporate elements into their own homes or their own designs. Equally important, he fostered the idea of the architect designer, the man who handled all details of his trade from the house right down to the knives and forks. Not that this was a new phenomenon; Pugin, after all, had done the same thing and after him others. Voysey continued the tradition, perhaps gave it some extra momentum and persuaded people a little more conclusively of the need to surround themselves with appropriate and beautiful things.

The Voysey house has come into our architectural language as a prototype and there are sufficient examples of it shown in the preceding pages for it not to be necessary again to offer a summary of its salient points. It was much copied, much adapted to suit particular needs; it has also been much debased in copying but that hardly matters. The man who produced it and the furniture and allied items that went with it combined the pleasing qualities of being truly distinctive and genuinely unassuming. More important, his work was outstanding and influential. From his personal qualities, his chosen manner of work and his achievement the picture that emerges is of an idiosyncratic talent and man which well fits him for the title of 'an architect of individuality'.

List of extant works

1888 The Cottage, Station Road, Bishop's Itchington, Warwicks, for M.H.Lakin. Addition 1900.

1890 Walnut Tree Farm, now Bannut Farm House, Castlemorton, nr Malvern, Heref. & Worcs., for R.H.Cazalet. With stables. Alterations 1894.

1890 Addition to The Cliff, 102 Coventry Road, Warwick, for M.H.Lakin.

1891 Studio at 17 St Dunstan's Road, London w6, for W.E.F.Britten. Extended at the rear since Voysey's time.

1891 14 South Parade, Bedford Park, London w4, for J.W.Forster. Addition 1894.

1891–2 14 and 16 Hans Road, London sw3, for Archibald Grove. Now offices and flats.

1893 Perrycroft, Jubilee Drive, Colwall, nr Malvern, Heref. & Worcs., for J.W.Wilson. Additions 1903–04 and 1907. Stables 1903, coachman's cottage 1908.

1894 Lowicks House, Sandy Lane, Tilford, nr Frensham, Surrey, for E.J.Horniman. Additions and alterations 1898, 1904, 1907 and 1911.

1895 Wentworth Arms Inn, Elmesthorpe, Hinckley, Leics., for the Earl of Lovelace.

1895 Annesley Lodge, Platt's Lane, London nw3, for the Revd Charles Voysey.

1896 Wortley Cottages, Elmesthorpe, Leics., for the Earl of Lovelace. Originally thatched but rebuilt by Voysey with slate roofs after fire, 1914.

1896 Greyfriars, The Hog's Back, nr Guildford, Surrey, for Julian Sturgis. With stables and lodge. Additions and alterations by H.Baker, 1913

1896 Hill Close, Studland Bay, Dorset, for A.Sutro. Recent alterations. Motor house and lodge for H.Cook, 1913.

1897 Norney Grange, nr Shackleford, Surrey, for the Revd W.Leighton Grane. With stables and lodge. Alterations and additions 1903.

1897 and 1899 Additions to Woodcote, Horsley, Surrey, for Sir Henry Roscoe.

1897 The Hill, Thorpe Mandeville, Northants., for Hope Brooke.

1897 New Place, Farnham Lane, Haslemere, Surrey, for A.M.M.Stedman, later Sir Algernon Methuen. Additions and alterations 1899 and 1901, including lodge, stables, summer house and additional formal garden.

1898 Broadleys, now The Motor Boat Club, Gillhead, nr Cartmel Fell, Lake Windermere, Lancs., for A.Currer Briggs. Stables 1900. Verandah filled in in recent times.

1898 Addition to 16 Chalcot Gardens, London nw3, for A.J.Whalley.

1898 Moor Crag, Gillhead, nr Cartmel Fell, Lake Windermere, Lancs. Stables 1900.

1899   Spade House, Radnor Cliff Crescent, Sandgate, Folkestone, Kent, for H.G.Wells. Additional storey 1903. Now an hotel.

1899   Beaworthy (now Winsford) Cottage Hospital, Halwill, Devon. Additions not by Voysey.

1899   Lodge at Bury Hill Park, Oldbury, Heref. & Worcs. Extensively altered since Voysey's time.

1899   Oakhill, 54 Oakhill Grove Crescent, Kidderminster, Heref. & Worcs., for F.J.Mayers.

1899   Oakhurst, now divided into two units called Ropes and Bollards, Ropes Lane, Fernhurst, Sussex, for Mrs E.F.Chester.

1899   The Orchard, Shire Lane, Chorleywood, Herts., for himself.

1900   Prior's Garth, now a school and called Priorsfield, Puttenham, Surrey, for F.H.Chambers. Additions by T.Müntzer, J.Brandon-Jones and Ashton and others.

1901   The Pastures, North Luffenham, Leics., for Miss G.Conant. Alterations and addition 1909.

1902   Addition to Roughwood Farm, Chalfont St Giles, Herts., for Captain Williams.

1902   Wallpaper factory, Barley Mow Passage, Chiswick, London w4, for Sanderson & Sons. Now offices.

1902   Vodin, now Little Court, Old Woking Road, Pyrford, Surrey, for F.Walters. Motor house and generating house 1904.

1902   Interior of dining-room including furniture at 37 Bidston Road, Birkenhead, Cheshire, for A.H.van Gruisen. Bedroom 1905. Furniture dispersed.

1902   Alterations, decoration and furniture at 30 Shrewbury Road, Birkenhead, Cheshire, for Miss McKay. Additional furniture 1909 and 1912. All furniture dispersed.

1903   Ty-bronna, St Fagan's Road, Fairwater, nr Cardiff, Glam., for W.Hastings Watson. Stables 1904. Alterations since Voysey's time. Now the property of the South Glamorgan Health Authority.

1903   White Cottage, 68 Lyford Road, London sw18, for C.T.Coggin. Additions since Voysey's time.

1903   Tilehurst, 10 Grange Road, Bushey, Herts., for Miss Somers.

1903   Hollybank, now Sunnybank, Shire Lane, Chorleywood, Herts., for Dr H.R.T.Fort, nominally for the Reverend Matthew Edmeades.

1904   Higham, Woodford, Essex, for Lady Henry Somerset. The house was built without Voysey's superintendence, and differs in several respects from his design.

1904   Myholme, Bushey, Herts., for Miss Somers. Built as a nursing home for children. Alterations 1911. Now a private house.

1904–5   Houses and Institute, Whitwood, nr Normanton, Yorks., for Henry Briggs & Son & Co. The houses were built without the architect's superintendence. The Institute is now The Rising Sun public house.

1905   White Horse Inn, now White Horse Stables, Stetchworth, Cambs., for the Earl of Ellesmere.

1905   Additions and alterations to Woodbrook, Alderley Edge, Cheshire, for A.Heyworth.

1905	Hollymount, Amersham Road, Knotty Green, Beaconsfield, Bucks., for C.T.Burke.
1905	The Homestead, Second Avenue, corner of Holland Road, Frinton-on-Sea, Essex, for S.C.Turner.
1906	Re-construction and furnishing at Garden Corner, 13 Chelsea Embankment, London sw3, for E.J.Horniman. Only a certain proportion of the fittings survive.
1906–10	Re-construction and furnishing offices of the Essex and Suffolk Equitable Insurance Company, Capel House, 54 and 62 New Broad Street, London ec2, for S.C.Turner. Only a small proportion of the fittings survive.
1906–7	Littleholme, Upper Guildown Road, Guildford, Surrey, for G.Müntzer. Now divided into two units. Gardener's cottage 1911
1906–7	Extensions and alterations and stables, coachman's cottage and gardener's cottage at Wilverley, now Highlands, Holtye Common, Sussex, for J.F.Goodhart.
1908	Grille for tomb at Kirby Mallory, Leics. and repairs to church for Lady Lovelace.
1909	Littleholme, 103 Sedbergh Road, Kendal, Cumbria, for A.W.Simpson.
1909	Holiday cottage at Slindon, Barnham Junction, Sussex, for A.A.Voysey.
1909	Brooke End, New Road, Henley-in-Arden, Warwicks., for Miss F.Knight.
1909	Lodge Style, Combe Down, near Bath, for T.S.Cotterell.
1910–11	The Old Barn, Holmbury St Mary, Surrey. Conversion of a barn into a convalescent home for F.J.Merrilees. Now converted into a house.
1911	House in Malone Road, Belfast, for Robert Hetherington.
1912	Lillycombe, Porlock, Somerset, for Lady Lovelace. Voysey made some alterations to a design by Lady Lovelace and supervised the execution of the work.
1913	Pleasure Ground, East Row, Kensal Green, London w10, for E.J.Horniman. This survives with some alterations.
1914	Re-modelling and extending White Cliffe, now High Gant, St Margaret's-at-Cliffe, Kent, for P.A.Barendt.
1919	War memorial at Malvern Wells, Heref. & Worcs.
1919	Alterations and additions to Hambledon Hurst, The Green, Hambledon, Surrey, for A.H.van Gruisen.
1919	Re-modelling a room in 29 Harley Street, London w1, for Leslie Paton.
1920	War memorial at Potters Bar, Herts.

Bibliography

Writings of C.F.A.Voysey

Reason as a basis of art, Elkin Mathews, London 1906
'Ideas in things' in *The Arts Connected with Building* (ed. T.Raffles Davison), Batsford, London 1909, pp.101–37
'Patriotism in architecture', *Architectural Association Journal*, XXVIII, 1912, pp.21–5
Individuality, Chapman & Hall, London 1915
Introduction to a catalogue of an exhibition of the work of C.F.A.Voysey at the Batsford Gallery, 1931

Writings on C.F.A.Voysey
British Publications

Aymer Vallance, 'The furnishing and decoration of the house: Part 2: walls, windows and stairs', *Art Journal*, LIV, 1892, pp.306–11
Anon., 'An Interview with Mr Charles F.Annesley Voysey, architect and designer', *Studio*, I, 1893, pp.231–7
E.B.S., 'Some recent designs by Mr C.F.A.Voysey', *Studio*, VII, 1896, pp.209–18
Anon., 'The Arts and Crafts Exhibition, 1896', *Studio*, IX, 1896, pp.190–6
Anon., 'Men who build: No.45: Mr Charles F.Annesley Voysey', *Builder's Journal & Architectural Record*, IV, 1896, pp.67–70
'G' 'The revival of English domestic architecture: the work of Mr C.F.A.Voysey', *Studio*, XI, 1897, pp. 16–25
E.B.S., 'Country cottages', *Country Life*, II, 1898, pp.195–7
Horace Townsend, 'Notes on country and suburban houses designed by C.F.A.Voysey', *Studio*, XVI, 1899, pp.157–64
Aymer Vallance, 'British decorative art in 1899 and the Arts and Crafts Exhibition', *Studio*, XVIII, 1899, pp.38–49, 185
Anon., 'Houses for people with hobbies: "The Orchard", Chorleywood', *Country Life*, VI, 1899, pp.389–90
Anon., 'Houses for people with hobbies: "Walnut Tree Farm", Castlemorton', *Country Life*, VI, 1899, pp.524–6
Charles Holme (ed.), *Modern British domestic architecture and decoration*, The Studio, London 1901, pp.181–94
T.Raffles Davison, 'The recent advances in architecture – country houses', *Magazine of Art*, n.s. I, 1903, pp.477–82
Anon., 'The Arts and Crafts Exhibition at the New Gallery', *Studio*, XXVIII, 1903, pp.28, 179
Maurice B.Adams, *Modern cottage architecture*, Batsford, London 1904, pp.7–8
W.Shaw Sparrow, *The British home of today*, Hodder & Stoughton, London 1904, after pp.54, 55, 64
Aymer Vallance, 'Some recent work by Mr C.F.A.Voysey', *Studio*, XXXI, 1904, pp.127–34
Anon., 'Some recent designs for domestic architecture', *Studio*, XXXIV, 1905, pp.151–2
J.H.Elder-Duncan, *Country cottages and weekend homes*, Cassell & Co., London 1906, pp.96–7, 186–7
W.Shaw Sparrow, *The Modern home*, Hodder & Stoughton, London 1906, pp.54, 55 & after p.64
A.B.Daryll, 'The architecture of Charles Francis Annesley Voysey', *Magazine of Fine Arts*, II, 1906, pp.191–6
Anon., 'The Orchard, a house', *Ideal House*, January 1907, pp.3–11
Mervyn E.Macartney, 'Recent English domestic architure', *Architectural Review*, London 1908, pp.171–3

T. Raffles Davison, *Modern Homes*, George Bell & Sons, London 1909, pp.20–1, 119–23

Lawrence Weaver, 'Small country houses of today', I, *Country Life*, London 1910, pp.139–44

Mervyn E. Macartney, 'Recent English domestic architecture', *Architectural Review*, London 1911, pp.167–72

Anon., 'C.F.A. Voysey: the man and his work', *Architect and Building News*, CXVII, 1927, pp.133–4, 219–21, 273–5, 314–16, 404–06

John Betjeman, 'Charles Francis Annesley Voysey, the architect of individualism', *Architectural Review*, LXX, 1931, pp.93–6

Marjorie & C.H.B. Quennell, *A history of everyday things in England*, IV, Batsford, London 1934, pp.106–07

P. Morton Shand, 'Scenario for a human drama: VII: looping the loop', *Architectural Review*, LXXVII, 1935, pp.99–104

Nikolaus Pevsner, *Pioneers of Modern Design*, Penguin, Harmondsworth 1949 (Original edn: *Pioneers of the modern movement*, Faber & Faber, London 1936), pp.141–54

J.M. Richards, *Architectural Review*, LXXXIX, 1941, pp.59–60 (obituary)

Nikolaus Pevsner, 'Charles F. Annesley Voysey, 1857–1941', *Architectural Review*, LXXXIX, 1941, pp.112–13

Howard Roberton & Noel D. Sheffield, *Journal of the Royal Institute of British Architects*, XLVIII, 1941, p.88 (obituary)

Anon., *Architects' Journal*, XCIII, pp.124 (obituary)

Robert Donat, 'Uncle Charles . . .', *Architects' Journal*, XCIII, 1941, pp.193–4

John Betjeman, 'C.F.A. Voysey', *Architects' Journal*, XCIII, 1941, pp.257–8

John Brandon-Jones, 'An Architect's letters to his client', *Architect & Building News*, CXCV, 1949, pp.494–8

John Brandon-Jones, *C.F.A. Voysey: a memoir*, Architectural Association, London 1957, reprint, Garland, New York 1977

Peter F. Floud, 'The wallpaper designs by C.F.A. Voysey', *Penrose Annual*, LII, 1958, pp.10–14

John Brandon-Jones, 'C.F.A. Voysey' in *Victorian Architecture* (ed. Peter Ferriday), Jonathan Cape, London 1963, pp.267–87

Margaret Richardson, 'Wallpapers by C.F.A. Voysey', *Journal of the Royal Institute of British Architects*, LXXII, 1965, pp.399–403

Nikolaus Pevsner, *Studies in art, architecture and design*, II, Thames & Hudson, London 1968, pp.186–9

Robert Macleod, *Style and society: architectural ideology in Britain 1836–1914*, RIBA, London 1971, pp.111–14

J. Morton, *Three generations in a family textile firm*, 1971, pp.96, 113–19, 177–8, 248–9, 286–7

John Brandon-Jones, 'Architects and the Art Workers' Guild', *Royal Society of Arts Journal*, CXXI, 1973, pp.192–203

Joanna Symonds, *Catalogue of Drawings by C.F.A. Voysey in the Drawings Collection of the Royal Institute of British Architects*, D.C. Heath Ltd/Gregg International, Farnborough, Hants. 1976

John Brandon-Jones and others, *C.F.A. Voysey: architect and designer 1857–1941*, Lund Humphries, London in association with Art Gallery and Museums and the Royal Pavilion, Brighton 1978. Contributors include Elizabeth Aslin, Shirley Bury, Joanna Heseltine, Barbara Morris and Duncan Simpson.

Writings on C.F.A. Voysey
Foreign Publications

Henri Van de Velde, 'Artistic wallpapers', *Emulations*, XVIII, Brussels 1893, pp.150–1

Henri Van de Velde, 'Essex and Co's Westminster wallpapers', *L'Art Moderne*, XIV, Brussels 1894, pp.253–4

F.E. von Bodenhausen, 'Englische Kunst im Hause', *Pan*, II, Berlin 1896–7, pp.329–36

Thiebault Sisson, 'L'art décoratif en Angleterre: "Arts and Crafts"', *Art et Décoration*, I, Paris 1897, pp.19–22

Anon., 'C.F.A. Voysey', *Dekorative Kunst*, I, Munich 1897, pp.241–80

M.P. Verneuil, 'Le papier-peint à l'exposition', *Art et Décoration*, VIII, 1900, pp.83–90

Edward W. Gregory, 'The Seventh exhibition of arts and crafts in London', *House & Garden*, III, New York 1903, pp.208–13

M.B., 'Some recent work of C.F.A. Voysey, an English architect', *House & Garden*, III, New York 1903, pp.255–60

Anon., 'Häuser von C.F.A. Voysey', *Der Baumeister*, Berlin March 1903, pp.61–4

Warren H. Langford, 'Recent domestic architecture in England', *Architectural Review* (Boston), XI, 1904, pp.5–12, 196

Hermann Muthesius, *Das englische Haus*, Ernst Wasmuth, 3 vols, Berlin 1904–5; *The English House*, translated by Janet Seligman, Crosby Lockwood Staples, Granada, London 1979 and Rizzoli, New York 1979

Hermann Muthesius, *Das moderne Landhaus*, Bruckmann, Munich 1905, pp.145–9, 190–1

Henry F.Ganz, 'Houses, Carnegie Library and Museum, textile designs', *Moderne Bauformen,* IV, Stuttgart 1905, pp.95–102, 106

J.Taylor, 'C.F.A.Voysey', *Upholstery Dealer & Decorative Furnisher,* VII, New York 1905, pp.19–26

P.G.Konody, 'C.F.A.Voyseys neuere Arbeiten', *Dekorative Kunst,* XIV, 1906, pp.193–8

Hermann Muthesius, *Landhaus und Garten*, Bruckmann, Munich 1907, pp.156–7

H.W.Frahne, 'Recent English domestic architecture', *Architectural Record,* XXV, New York 1909, pp.259–70

Paul Klopfer, 'Voyseys Architektur-Idyllen', *Moderne Bauformen,* IX, Stuttgart 1910, pp.141–8

Anon., 'Special Furniture', *Craftsman,* XX, New York 1911, pp.476–86

C.H.Boer, 'C.F.A.Voyseys Raumkunst', *Moderne Bauformen,* X, Stuttgart 1911, pp.247–56

The Craftsman, XXIII, New York 1912, pp.174–82

Nikolaus Pevsner, '1860–1930', *Architectural Record,* LXXXI, New York March 1937, pp.2–3

Anon., 'C.F.A.Voysey's eightieth birthday', *Deutsche Tapeten-Zeitung,* 1 June 1937

John Betjeman, 'C.F.A.Voysey', *Architectural Forum,* LXXII, New York 1940, pp.348–9

Kay Fisker, 'Tre pionerer fra aarhundredskiftet: C.F.A.Voysey, M.H.Baillie Scott, H. Tessenow', *Byggmästeren,* XXVI, 1947

Julius Posener, *Anfänge des Funktionalismus*, Ullstein, Berlin 1964, pp.71–94

Julius Posener, 'Il funzionalismo cominicia in Inghilterra', *Edilizia Moderna,* No.80, 1965, pp.54–64

Henry-Russell Hitchcock, 'English architecture in the early twentieth century: 1900–1939', *Zodiac,* XVIII, Rome 1968, pp.6–9

David Gebhard, *Charles F.A.Voysey, Architect*, Henessy & Ingalls, Los Angeles 1975

Notes

Chapter 1

1 *C.F.A.Voysey, A Memoir*, by John Brandon-Jones, ARIBA, AADipl, (Architectural Association, London 1957)

Catalogue of the Drawings Collection of the Royal Institute of British Architects – C.F.A.Voysey, (Gregg International, London 1975) by Joanna Symonds with an Introduction, 'Charles Francis Annesley Voysey' (pp.7–10) by John Brandon-Jones

C.F.A.Voysey – Architect and Designer, 1857–1941 (Lund Humphries/Art Gallery and Museums and the Royal Pavilion, Brighton, 1978) with an Introduction by John Brandon-Jones, pp.9–24

2 *C.F.A.Voysey, A Memoir*, op.cit., from the section entitled 'Practice' (the pages are un-numbered)

3 ibid.

4 *Three Generations in a Family Textile Firm* (Routledge and Kegan Paul 1971) by Jocelyn Morton

5 *Studio*, vol.1, no.6, Sept. 1893, pp.231–7, 'An Interview with Mr Charles F.Annesley Voysey, architect and designer', p.233

6 *Architects Journal*, XCIII, 1941, pp.193–4, 'Uncle Charles' by Robert Donat

7 *British Architect*, LXXIII, March 4 1910, p.160

8 *Catalogue of an Exhibition of the Works of C.F.A.Voysey*, for an exhibition held at the Batsford Gallery, Oct. 1931 – from the Foreword by Sir Edwin Lutyens (reprinted *Architectural Review*, vol.70, 1931, p.91)

9 *Architectural Review*, vols 89–90, March 1941, p.60, Obituary notice by J.M. (now Sir James) Richards

Chapter 2

1 *Studio*, vol.1, no.6, Sept. 1893, pp.231–7

2 *Studio*, vol.XI, no.51, June 1897, pp. 16–25

3 *British Architect*, vol.XXXI, 1889: 'Design for a Tower House', p.70; 'Design for a House with an Octagonal Hall', facing p.248

4 *Studio*, vol.XI, no.51, June 1897, p.25

5 *Black Book* – an account by Voysey, very brief in detail and also to some extent retrospective, of his projects and work; this account is not totally reliable. A typical entry might give a date, name of client, indication of location and perhaps a few details of the nature of the job

6 'Simple Furniture' by W.R.Lethaby from a volume entitled *Plain Handicrafts* (Percival and Co., London, 1892)

7 *Journal of the RIBA*, vol.1, 3rd series, 1894: 'Domestic Furniture', transcription of a lecture given to the RIBA General Meeting by Voysey, 23 April 1894. Quotations are from pp.416, 417 and 417 respectively

8 *Double Lives* by William Plomer, an autobiography (1st edn 1943); quoted from Jonathan Cape edn 1950, pp.99–100

Chapter 3

1 *Studio*, vol.XXI, no.94, Jan. 1901, pp.242–6; quoted from p.242

2 ibid., p.243

3 ibid., p.244

4 ibid., p.244

5 *Studio*, vol.IV, no.22, Jan.1895, p.128

6 *Studio*, vol.XXV, no.108, March 1902, p.86

7 ibid.

8 *The Mansions of England in the Olden Times* (The Studio, 1906) by Joseph Nash; the new edition edited by Charles Holme with a substantial Introduction by the architect Charles Harrison Townsend. Published from the original 4 vol. edition of 1838–49

9 *Journal of the RIBA*, vol.I, 3rd series, 1894, 'Domestic Furniture', transcription of a lecture given to the RIBA General Meeting by Voysey, 23 April 1894; p.417

10 ibid., p.417

11 *Artist*, Oct. 12, 1896, pp.9–40, Special No., 'Arts and Crafts Exhibition', p.21

12 *Studio*, vol.IX, no.45, Dec. 1896, p. 194

13 *Studio*, vol.VII, no.38, May 1896, pp.209–219, 'Some Recent Designs by Mr Voysey', p.216

14 ibid., p.217

15 *Journal of Decorative Art*, vol.XV, 1895, pp.82–90: 'The Aims and Conditions of the Modern Decorator'

16 *Studio*, vol.IX, no.45, Dec. 1896, 'The Arts and Crafts Exhibition, 1896', p.192

17 ibid., p.196

Chapter 4

1 *Das englische Haus* (Ernst Wasmuth, Berlin, 1904–5, 3 vols) by Hermann Muthesius; *The English House*, translated by Janet Seligman (Crosby Lockwood Staples, Granada, London 1979 and Rizzoli, New York 1979)

2 *Studio*, vol.XVI, no.73, April 1899, pp.157–64, 'Notes on Country and Suburban Houses designed by C.F.A.Voysey', by Horace Townsend, p.162

3 The correspondence is reproduced in full in *Architect and Building News*, vol.CXCV, 3 June 1949, pp.494–8, 'An Architect's Letters to his Client', by John Brandon-Jones

4 ibid.

5 *Studio*, op.cit., pp.161–2

6 *Architect and Building News*, op.cit.

7 ibid.

8 all ibid.

9 *Country Life*, vol.6, Sept. 30 1899, pp.389–90, from p.389

10 *Studio*, vol.XXIV, no.105, Dec. 1901, pp.162–72, 'Bournville, a Study in Housing Reform', p.172

Chapter 5

1 *Architectural Association Notes*, vol.XIX, no.207, May 1904, pp.71–73, 'On Craftsmanship', p.73

2 *Individuality* (Chapman and Hall, London 1915) by C.F.A.Voysey, pp.115–6

3 *British Architect*, LXXV, Jan. 27 1911, 'The English Home' by C.F.A.Voysey, pp.60 and 69–70; transcription of a paper read to the Design Club, Jan. 11 1911; quoted from p.69

4 *The Arts Connected with Building* (Batsford, London 1909) ed. T.Raffles Davison: 'Ideas in Things', pp.101–37, by C.F.A.Voysey. Quoted from p.115

5 ibid., p.115

6 ibid., p.120

7 ibid., p.136

8 ibid., p.130

9 ibid., p.130

Chapter 6

1   *Builder*, CXXV, 1923, pp.990–1

2   *Houses and Gardens* (George Newnes, London 1906) by M.H.Baillie Scott, pp.116–8

3   ibid., p.116

4   ibid., p.116

Chapter 7

1   *Das englische Haus* (Ernst Wasmuth, Berlin 1904–5) by Hermann Muthesius; quoted from the English edition; *The English House* (Crosby Lockwood Staples, Granada, London 1979 and Rizzoli, New York 1979) p.43

2   *Individuality* (Chapman and Hall, London 1915) by C.F.A.Voysey

3   ibid., p.142

4   ibid., pp.62–3

5   ibid., p.63

6   ibid., p.63

7   ibid., p.100

8   ibid., pp.107–8

9   *British Architect*, LXXIII, March 4 1910, pp.148–61, a paper read to the Carpenters Company by C.F.A.Voysey, p.148

10 *RIBA Journal*, vol.XXX, no.7, 10 Feb. 1923, a letter by C.F.A. Voysey, p.211

11 *British Architect*, LXXV, 27 Jan. 1911, pp.60 and 69–70, 'The English Home' by C.F.A.Voysey; transcription of a paper read to the Design Club, 11 Jan. 1911; quoted from p.60

12 ibid., p.60

13 *Journal of Decorative Art*, vol.XV, April 1895, pp.82–8, from a lecture delivered at the City Art Gallery, Manchester, p.83

14 *British Architect*, as 11 above, p.60

Index of buildings and designs

Voysey's houses are listed under their names and also under their locations. Unnamed houses are listed under place names. The 'List of extant works' on pp.149–151 provides the names of Voysey's clients, for quick reference.